OH NO!

MY WONDER WOMAN CAPE IS CAUGHT IN THE VACUUM!

A woman's guide to living a purpose-filled, balanced life.

BY

RUTH WHEAT AND BRENDA VICENTE

Cover Illustration and Design by Belinda Hamilton

Printed in the United States of America

Email:info@ruthwheatauthorspeaker.com

www.ruthwheatauthorspeaker.com

ISBN 979-8-89546-187-7

Library of Congress Control Number: 2011903785

10987654321

FOR ALL THE WOMEN WHO HAVE EVER WORN
THE WONDER WOMAN CAPE

FOREWORD

If you met Ruth and Brenda in person, you'd notice that they have a palpable vibrancy and an intense adoration for women, the moment they are in their presence.I've never known two more passionate women.They want to watch you fly and help you cultivate your own wind that will keep you aloft."Help! My Wonder Woman Cape is Caught in the Vacuum!" is based upon lessons they learned while living their roles as wife, mom, sister, friend and corporate executive.They share these lessons from their hearts.Enjoy the read!You'll be glad you did!

Chelsea Ryan Braun

ACKNOWLEDGMENTS

These pages are dedicated to the women who have been our role models and greatest champions.Our mothers, Kathleen Buras and Gail Powers taught us that we can be whoever we want and that having personal power doesn't preclude gentleness and kindness.

Their families came first, they had dinner on the table every night at the same time, and they gave more of themselves than they often had to give.We patterned our lives after theirs; trying to become the Wonder Woman we believed them to be.

We have both been blessed with the joys and pains of motherhood and our goal is to give our daughters, Ashlee, Chelsea, and Kacie, the same legacy that we've had, but we know that the Wonder Woman Cape can be overpowering at times.We desire to encourage them to choose what's most important to them and realize that when they choose to follow their dreams and live passionate, purpose-filled lives, they will enrich their lives and the lives of others around them.

This book would not have been written without our close friendship.After all, we believe we are "sisters from another mother."From every word we wrote to every Lucy and Ethel moment we've shared; we will treasure this experience for a lifetime.

To:

Buck Wheat and Joe Vicente,

the Super-Men in our lives,

thanks for the encouragement and support

during our journey,

all the women who generously shared their thoughts and stories,
which make this book so rich,

and

the Wonderous Women

who take off their Wonder Woman Capes

and live a life of passion and purpose.

WELCOME TO OUR REVISED EDITION!

Ruth and Brenda published the original version of "Help! My Wonder Woman Cape is Caught in the Vacuum!" in 2011.In the past thirteen years, a lot has happened!Brenda's daughter was 18 and Ruth's daughters were 25 and 33. All the daughters are now married and have blessed us with wonderful sons-in-law and lovely grandchildren.

Ruth and Brenda retired from the staffing industry and began living the retirement lifestyle.Though they love being retired, they stay busy!In fact, Brenda says she stays busier now than when she was working!

Brenda's life in Tennessee is wonderfully full and active. From managing real estate properties to staying fit at the gym, she keeps herself busy. Traveling with her husband adds a touch of adventure to their lives. The joy of weekly gatherings with friends and family brings everyone closer, creating cherished memories. And of course, the delight of having three beautiful grandchildren makes life even more special for Brenda and Joe.

Ruth and her husband moved to the Sam Houston National Forest and live in a log home at the lake.She is actively involved in a neighborhood ladies' Bible Study, plans and coordinates ladies' retreats, goes on fun adventures with her husband Buck, and continues to write, recently publishing "Giddy Up, Estelle! We've got a lot of living to do!!" One of her most cherished roles is that of "Mia" to her 7 grandchildren!

Their stories are a testament to the beauty of balance, the power of love, living our passion, and the joy of community. Even though the road has been bumpy at times they have tried to make the most of every moment and cherish the journey. Remember, the journey is not always perfect, it is the destination that matters.

The concept of letting go of the Wonder Woman cape and becoming the Wonderous Woman we are created to be, has not changed.The world may look a bit different, but women still face the same type of challenges that existed in 2011.

This edition also features Ruth and Brenda's daughters sharing some advice with their peers.

Enjoy the read and let go of the cape!

TABLE OF CONTENTS

INTRODUCTION

Why are we writing this book?Easy "Wonder Woman" is tired!

As women, we fulfill many roles and many of us seem to have an innate desire to be perfect at all of them.Striving for perfection in just one role - wife, mother, housekeeper, daughter, sister, employee, volunteer, or friend can be a full-time job.Somewhere along the way, a lot of us donned a Wonder Woman cape (thank goodness one size fits all) and jumped heart-first into a life of constant demands.If you have ever felt like you are being "sucked in" and can't escape – you may be one of "us."

Fortunately (or not) many women are experts at multi-tasking and can often make everything work – for a while.But what about the woman we are inside?Who makes sure she is getting nurtured?Are her dreams ever a priority?Is she experiencing opportunities to fuel her passions?Is her life balanced or in constant chaos?

We've spoken to women around the globe and have found a common denominator – the desire to live a purpose-filled, balanced life. Interestingly, most of them quickly related to the Wonder Woman fantasy.

> *"Ah, Wonder Woman.She had it all, didn't she?Great looks, a fabulous job that she could do well because she had superpowers to help her and was a great-looking sidekick.*

Unfortunately, most of us don't have superpowers.Most of us skate along as best we can with what Nature gave us, feeling guilty because we can't do it all. I finally got old enough to stop feeling guilty.

I don't wonder if Wonder Woman developed out of the feminist era.We were told we could do anything a man could do, including climb the corporate ladder. Unfortunately, somewhere along the way that got translated into "should" and "must" climb the corporate ladder.We felt a responsibility to make the climb to prove that our mothers were right.We began juggling our careers with motherhood and elder care, and since we also grew up in the sexual revolution, we also feel the need to be fabulous lovers and wives.Many of us burned out, having no free time to be ourselves and pursue our dreams."

Janet Lentz

Greater Philadelphia Area

These comments have been echoed by woman after woman.So, the desire to write this book was born.

It is our hearts' desire that when you finish reading this book, you will be reacquainted with the girl you are inside, encouraged to nurture your passions and dreams, find balance among the roles you love - and send Wonder Woman back to the comic books!We want you to fully connect to the Wonderous Woman God created you to be.

Getting the most from this experience

We will be giving you some thought-provoking questions to consider, and simple, yet stimulating exercises to guide you through a journey of self-discovery.Having a journal ready to jot down your thoughts will greatly enrich your experience.And, if you're like us, you may need to recall information that sometimes gets lost in the shuffle of our day-to-day lives.

Oh, and by the way, treat yourself to a beautiful journal – your thoughts deserve a special place.We've created a journal entitled "My Wonderous Woman Journal" that can be found on Amazon.com and provides you with pages that coincide with the journaling suggestions we make in the book.

Beginning your journey

Today begins this exciting journey.Give yourself the gift of time to experience the emotions that may surface as you read each page.We guess that you'll laugh and cry, but our wish is that you experience joy as you nurture your spirit.Enjoy!

Ruth Wheat

Brenda Vicente

CHAPTER 1
WHO IS WONDER WOMAN?

Wonder Woman was created by Dr. William Moulton Marston (writer) and Harry Peter, (artist).She first appeared in All Star Comics in 1944 close on the heels of superheroes Superman and Batman.

Marston wanted to create a superhero that would save the world with love vs. power.Elizabeth, William's wife, thought this was a great idea and insisted that the superhero be a woman. (Makes a lot of sense since we tend to be superheroes, we might as well get the recognition!) Elizabeth, in Marston's eyes, was a model of the unconventional, liberated woman of the era.It was during this same World War II era that other characters such as Rosie the Riveter were created to encourage women to see themselves as valuable beyond the roles of homemaker and mother - including working outside the home.

Marston fashioned the Wonder Woman character using characteristics from both his wife Elizabeth and Olive Byrne, a former student, with whom Marston was involved in an intimate relationship while married to Elizabeth.Elizabeth was the model of that era's unconventional liberated woman, while Olive was known to be the influence of Wonder Woman's appearance. Olive bore a striking resemblance to the Wonder Woman character and the heavy Indian bracelets she wore on each wrist gave rise to Wonder Woman's bracelets with special powers.Both Elizabeth and Olive bore children to Marston and Olive stayed home with the children while Elizabeth went off to work.We find it interesting that it took the characteristics of two women to create the Wonder Woman persona.

As a member of the all-female Amazon tribe, Wonder Woman was created as a distinctly feminist role model.Her mission was to bring the Amazon ideals of love, peace and sexual equality to a "world torn by the hatred of men."Her skills include super strength, super speed, super stamina, super agility and flight.In other words, she is the "queen" of multitasking and moves at warped speed!Sound familiar?

To keep the superhero "approachable" they always seem to have an alter-ego.Superman has mild-mannered reporter Clark Kent; Batman has Bruce Wayne; and even Wonder Woman has an alter ego – Diana Prince.The superhero identity emerges only when they need it to.They don't use their superpowers 24/7.Somehow, though, the idea of Wonder Woman as a role model for contemporary women seems to have evolved into a way of life.As we get busier and more pressures are put on us, we seem to have taken her mission on as a full-time job.Only… we don't have a separate identity to step into when things get crazy!In many respects, we take on the Wonder Woman mission unknowingly, and then one day the subconscious is jolted into reality.

We even have support for this model in the media. Watching television has influenced how women see themselves in the roles of wife and mother.We also observed as families navigated their day-to-day lives and often judged our own lives by theirs.

In the 1950's and 1960's June Cleaver was introduced as a stay-at-home mom who was immaculate.She had two boys, one of whom was a hot mess.He was always up to some kind of mischief. June navigated his escapades with the help of his brother, Wally, and her husband, Ward.She was always perfect, wore pearls and heels to vacuum, and had healthy, balanced dinners on the table every night like clockwork.

The 1970's brought us Happy Days, which was set in the 1950s, where the matriarch Marion was learning to deal with teenagers and all of the drama and shenanigans they were involved in. Marion was also a stay-at-home mom some thought to be ditzy, but she wasn't ditzy at all.She had so many things on her mind (sound familiar?) She was in fact way ahead of everybody and running everything that was going on!

Television shows during the 1980s shared a version of families that were very different from sitcoms in the 1970s. For example, Florence Henderson brought Carol Brady to life as the perfect mom and stepmom, successfully blending a family of 6 children, a dog, a cat, a bossy housekeeper, and a usually perplexed and pliable husband. In 1984 the hit comedy, The Cosby Show launched, and Claire Huxtable taught us many mother lessons She was a busy, classy woman, a successful attorney, mother of five and wife to Cliff (which was a full-time job all in itself).We were never introduced to a housekeeper, but we are convinced she had one!Her assertive, no-nonsense nature allowed her children to grow up happy and healthy. Throughout these decades, the women of TV were all able to get things done regardless of everything going on around them.Regardless of whether you were born in the Boomer, Generation X, or Millennial generation, you've probably been influenced by the concept of some of these women.

The desire to become Wonder Woman and the perfect wife and mother has evolved.A poll, conducted during the research period of this book, showed that contemporary women have definite opinions about the Wonder Woman persona within us.Here are a few of their thoughts…

> *"She is married, middle-aged, has two teens, 3 dogs, 3 cats, and 8 fish, runs her own business from home, cooks meals for her family, attends college two nights per week, volunteers for School programs, runs errands, provides transportation for the kids and their friends, keeps the house clean, organizes special events for the family, does her marketing, takes care of all the physical needs of her entire family including the pets. Volunteers time at church as*

needed and attends church 2 times per week. She has a 17-year-old boy who is now driving and getting ready for college in August. She helps with all the paperwork for college and transports her son's girlfriend when in need. She takes her other child to after-school activities. Did I mention she does laundry, shops for groceries, and whatever else is needed?She provides excellent service to her clients, is honest – and tired!"

Michelle Cardenas, Orange County, CA

"I think that every woman has the potential to be a Wonder Woman for a time, but there comes a day when she has to pull the bobby pins out of her hair, rip off her pantyhose, throw on some sweats and say, "enough is enough--I need to regain my balance!" Only when we have gotten to that point of overload are we going to truly discover our inner "superpowers," and be able to perform to our best – not fullest or most-crammed-in –but to our BEST abilities."

Candice Lange, Toledo OH

I grew up in a generation that was told that we could "have it all." And I believed it. So now I'm the primary breadwinner in the family. I do all of the housework. I take care of the car. I do our taxes. I have a career and throw dinner parties for my husband's friends. And afterward, I clean up. I have it all -- and it's freakin' exhausting!!!!"

Kay Lorraine, Honolulu HI

These are just three of the hundreds of like responses we received.Do these responses represent a fairly universally held set of feelings?We have to ask: "What do we think being Wonder Woman will get us?"There must be a payoff, or we would not keep doing this.

For many of us being known as "Wonder Woman" feeds our self-esteem.So often, we attach our self-worth to what we do.We have been led to believe that we should be able to "get everything done" and when we don't - there's "something wrong with us."

We all know women who appear to have it all.They look great, their kids are great, they win the "Volunteer of the Year" award, they get recognized for their contributions at work, their houses are beautifully decorated, and their clothes are perfectly in style.

These expectations aren't realistic.

> *"When I met the man who would become my husband, I figured I could squeeze in marriage because I had Tuesday evenings free!*
>
> *Between my very full-time job in which I traveled a great deal, teaching scuba diving, leading scuba trips, heading the stewardship campaign at church, and wearing a zillion other volunteer hats, it seemed reasonable to fit this one more thing in! But he didn't cooperate in taking only Tuesday evenings and weekend evenings.*
>
> *Later when the question of children came up, I thought about adding that to my 2-hour commute each way each day, my very full-time job, my graduate program, my volunteer activities, and my other family commitments, I realized that I was NOT Wonder Woman.The whole concept of Wonder Woman is such a travesty that we (have) foisted on women!In our quest for liberation, we created this no-win expectation for everyone!"*
>
> **Pegotty Cooper, Tampa FL**

The wisdom apparent in these women's testimonies reflects the awareness of a disconnect between the truly special and gifted person that we are, and the super-human expectations we set for ourselves.A part of us always knows that the comic book Wonder Woman and the TV super-mom are fiction.However, some models are more difficult to overlook and dismiss.

Wisdom literature from all ages holds the ideal woman to a standard with which all of us would love to identify – and, which many of us will do anything to live up to.

In a quiet moment of sane reflection, we have to ask ourselves, "What does being Wonder Woman get us?"Looking at our lives, the answer is pretty clear.Feeling overwhelmed, anxiety, low self-esteem, depression, stress, and physical illnesses are just some of the byproducts of trying to be Wonder Woman.

Within days of announcing the title of this book, we received hundreds of emails resonating with this challenge.The responses above and those that will appear throughout the book make it clear that we recognize there is a painful and damaging gap between "who we want to be" (wanting it all), and "having balance" (and how we are going to get it).

You must wonder, "How does Wonder Woman get it all done?"She never goes insane!She always pulls off every challenge!!!

HOW DOES SHE DO THAT???

Again, we can take some comfort in knowing that Wonder Woman is fiction.Certainly, Diana Prince didn't fulfill all those expectations and get all of it done.She knew that call was "beyond her identity as Diana Prince."But then there's that pesky proverb and centuries of tradition extolling the mountain of things a woman can do – as Ginger Rogers so aptly observed, "She did everything Fred Astaire did… except backward and in high heels." Geez!!

"Life Balance" is what we are trying to achieve… while at the same time, a journey of self-fulfillment.

So… we have identified the problem.But what is the solution?

CHAPTER 2
THE WONDER OF YOU

We all know ourselves pretty well. After all, we've known ourselves all our lives.We know our good qualities and our bad.Our innermost thoughts are only privy to ourselves.And though we know the really great things about ourselves, we tend to focus our attention on areas that we don't like.We can become overwhelmed at times with our flaws.Is it any wonder then, that our desire to escape into Wonder Woman is a way to escape our true identity?Sometimes we are afraid that the real person we are inside may not be good enough.

When we learn to look beyond our flaws and recognize the unique gifts we have, then we can celebrate the wonder of who we are.We can truly love ourselves, regardless of our flaws. And we'll find that our flaws become part of our uniqueness and charm. This idea is best illustrated by the great children's story of "The Velveteen Rabbit."

With "most of his fur loved off" and even missing an eye, this endearing symbol of devotion and love has transfixed generations of readers who would not part with their "Velveteen Rabbit Memory" for a thousand new, fluffy bunny toys.

What would the pressures of your life be like – if you loved you – like most of us love "The Velveteen Rabbit?"This is not only possible… it is the answer.

The WONDER of YOU

Past the basic appearances – no two of us who are alive now or who have ever been alive, are alike.We are unique individuals both physically and personally.Ask any parent of identical twins.They will tell you.They are not the same!In the fourth month of pregnancy, the fingerprints of the fetus are formed.Much earlier than that, the combined DNA of the fertilized egg specifies the individual that will emerge.The code is stamped, one that never appeared before and will never appear again!

Attitudes, outlook, and gifts – all are unique to each of us.Just as we've all met someone and envied their gifts or talent, there is also someone in the world who would look at us and covet the cards we have been dealt and how we've played them.

Why don't we value our gifts?Familiarity with our imperfections plays a part.But also, most of us are taught early on not to brag or celebrate our specialness – not to get the "big head" – not to be arrogant.We all have little victories as children that others can celebrate about us… but that we are not to celebrate ourselves.We become so absorbed in trying not to be self-absorbed that we forget who we were made to be.

We're inundated with messages that we aren't okay like we are.Pay attention to commercials during prime time. You're only sexy if you can fit into a pair of tight jeans and look like a model in them. When we turned 25 and suddenly became a target market for face cream, peels and masks we thought if we didn't buy them our skin would sag overnight!We know we need to lose 10 pounds, but we don't want to be reminded at every commercial break.We're trying to "learn how to love the skin we're in" but those diet commercials won't let us!

Here is the bottom line:

- Bragging and arrogance are not self-love - they are fear of being unloved.

- Self-appreciation comes not from what you do or how you look but from who you are.
- Who you are is: A child of God.
- God makes everything and everyone for a reason.
- God made you with a purpose.
- Your purpose is as unique to you as your DNA.
- Your purpose may have nothing to do with what you do.
- Your purpose cannot be fulfilled by anyone else.

As you can see, we are amazing women whom God chose to live our lives with value and purpose.You may be thinking, “sounds good, but I have a lot of doubts sometimes about my value and worth.”Finding self-appreciation and self-love may seem hard but friends, it is one of the best gifts you can give yourself.

Today, social media has developed our perception of value by the number of “friends” and “likes” we have.Sounds crazy, right?!This version of value and worth is completely outward-focused – what others think of us.

Girls, it has to come from within.A friend of ours was looking in the mirror trying to identify characteristics that she appreciated about herself.She decided that she had pretty great earlobes!And you know what?She does!

We’d like to challenge you to the practice of looking for things you like about yourself every day.Come on - you know you have a cute nose or a wonderful pout.Get started today!

It doesn’t have to be big things!Sheryl Crow, an American musician, pointed out this truth in one of her songs “Soak Up the Sun”, Joy is “not having what you want, but wanting what you have”. The ancient wisdom in play here is: “It is not the joyful who are grateful – but the grateful who are joyful!” Our friend found a day to be grateful for earlobes.Ruth found a day when the freckles weren't a curse but a blessing.Brenda found a day when she realized that her 5-foot almost 1-inch frame has some benefits after all!

So, take time to write to respond to these five sentence starters.Leave lots of room to come back later and fill in newly discovered joys.Make it your goal to fill that big space over time – and to run out of room for things to write down for which you are grateful.Then on a day when the earlobes don't look so perfect, review your responses and remind yourself of the Wonderous Woman that you were created to be.

I love it when I...

____

____

____

____

I'm really good at...

____

____

____

____

My favorite feature is ...

____

____

____

People tell me that I…

____

____

____

____

I am so proud of… (remember, this isn't about your kids or your family, it's about you!)

____

____

____

____

These exercises are very practical.They can change your life if you let them.Your training in self-ignoring may be so well planted that this process not only does not come naturally to you – it may even be hard.Here is a suggestion that we urge you to try at least once.Tell a friend you have homework to do, and you are stuck.Ask her to help you answer a few questions listed above.You will find she has much less trouble than you.Just as you may have no trouble at all filling in these blanks – for her!There is a wonderful story that has made the rounds on the internet that demonstrates the importance of being aware of our positive uniqueness.

An elementary school teacher – let us call her Mrs. Curtis – decided one day to task her rowdy and restless class of third graders with writing down the names of all their classmates.Then they took the rest of the afternoon to write one sentence about each of them, but it had to be a sentence describing one thing about that person that they liked.At the day's end she collected the papers and over the weekend put each student's name on an individual sheet of paper and transcribed every positive sentence for that student onto the page.

On Monday she distributed the pages and gave the students time to read.First, they were silent.Then the smiles began.Then, they began looking around the room wondering "who likes my eyes?"There was a change in the class after that but more importantly, a change in each child.They were valued.By every other person in their class!

That could be the end of the story – but it isn't.Years later the teacher received a phone call. The news was hard."Mrs. Curtis, this is John Stenson's father.He was in your class in third grade.Mrs. Curtis, John is coming home from Vietnam.Next Tuesday is his funeral."John's father asked if she would be at the funeral and, of course, she agreed.

At the service, his best friend eulogized John and then mentioned that while going through his belongings he had found a paper with a list of things people had liked about him.It was old and worn and he'd carried it for a long time.He said that he liked those things about John also.

Mrs. Curtis was, of course, deeply moved.But her day was not over.After the service, she found that four other attendees were her students from that class.Each still had their own paper.Each re-read it often.Particularly, when they doubted their value.

We all need to be reminded of how special we are to others. Through the years, Ruth has kept cards that she's received for sentimental reasons.

> *"A few years ago, I ran across my box of cards and began rereading them.I had received notes from my friends, family, co-workers, people who had attended classes that I taught, and my managers.As I read the notes, my heart was filled with joy, and I realized that these people valued me and my gifts.I began keeping notes that I received after that very intentionally.Each note, email, and card were placed in my newly named "Smile File".This file is precious.Whenever I feel self-doubt or I'm going through a particularly difficult*

time, I reach for my "Smile File." And I end up smiling!I recommend that you give this idea a try – it will touch your soul!"

Those who love us know our value.They have no doubt.Find time every day to express gratitude for who you are and the gift that you are.We should be among those who love us – and are certain of our value.It is not arrogance or conceit.It reminds us that we were fearfully and wonderfully made – for a reason.

The Value of a Purpose

We hear the word "purpose" a lot these days.So, what is purpose?Our "Life's Purpose" is who God created us to be.Discovering, understanding, and living our purpose expresses who we really are.It shapes our choices and becomes evident in what we do.But what we do is not our purpose. The effect our life has on those whose lives we touch – that is our purpose.

From world-famous celebrities who can't wait to be in front of the camera to the person who truly enjoys cutting your hair or the teenager who has dedicated her life to dance and the mom who home-schools her children - we can find people every day who are "On Purpose."They are living the life they were born to live.

A life lived with purpose will affect more lives than we might ever imagine.One of the greatest role models for living a life of purpose was Mother Teresa.By worldly standards, she lived a simple, humble, even meager life.She even found joy in cleaning toilets. Just by showing love and compassion, she touched the lives of the poor, unknown, and unlovable who stood before her and in so doing, she touched millions of lives around the world.The exciting notion here is that we each have our purpose – we don't have to be like someone else.We each have our unique talents and gifts.Every purpose has value – and that value may live on and be our legacy.

Getting Back to the Girl Inside

When we think back to when we were little girls, we remember that we were filled with a sense of wonder, didn't take ourselves seriously, and were full of playfulness.We spent time dreaming.And then we grew up. All those daydreams had been filled with promise.What happened to them?Practical (fearful) adults taught us to be "realistic."Some of us were lucky enough to have role models in our lives to support our dreams.Regardless, we grew up and often put our dreams aside or on hold for the more practical demands we seemed to see before us.How has that worked out?

We took a few moments and thought back to our childhood and reacquainted ourselves with the little girls we were.What a great experience.

Ruth's story:

"I remember wanting to be on a stage as a famous singer.I loved the idea of entertaining large groups of people and wearing beautiful evening gowns.As the oldest of five children, I also took advantage of my leadership skills and directed neighborhood plays based on fairy tales.My entrepreneurial spirit engaged early as I found a way to charge for admission!Though it was only a nickel, that was something!

As I grew older, I was involved in opportunities that gave me a chance to sing.But early on, I recognized that there were a lot of people that were as good as, and better than I.My self-confidence waivered some.I was fortunate that my mother supported any ideas and dreams that we had, but I didn't have any role models in the area of music to follow.I let my own limiting beliefs hold me back.I played it safe, sang in church (they have to like you there, right?), and set out to become a teacher.Becoming a teacher didn't materialize either – I entered the business world.I've been very fortunate in that eventually I found myself on a stage entertaining a lot of people as a speaker – a teacher!My original desire to be a singer was based upon my understanding of folks who I saw on stage – singers!Who knew that I would experience the desire of my heart without singing a note?! Gratefully, my heavenly Father knew exactly what I was to do

Brenda's story:

"As a little girl, I loved to play "house", take care of my baby dolls, and dream of happily ever after. Being the only girl in the family, I would often convince my younger brother to play along with me, but his interest was short-lived. My parents owned a business, which sparked my interest in playing office games. I would alternate between being the boss and the secretary, depending on my brother's willingness to participate.

My childhood dreams of being a mother and working in a business came true. My passion for business led me to become the President and COO of a national, $300M firm. All the practice I had as a child paid off, and I achieved those childhood goals

As children, our dreams were based upon the limited knowledge that we had.As we grew up, we added to our dreams, and some of those dreams we achieved while others faded, or we just settled for "something less."We believe that we should never stop dreaming.We need to approach dreaming today as we did as children – full of possibilities and the belief that anything can come true.Dreaming is such an important part of life that we devoted Chapter 5 to the topic.

The argument that comes up here is that, as adults, it is time to quit dreaming, get real, and move out of the fantasy world.Where did that come from?We believe that the cause is based on the societal demands to achieve as well as the fear of failure.So, we bottled up those dreams and focus on the current demands in our lives.

So, if the circumstances of your life are saying "play it safe" and the heart in the center of your spirit is saying "this stuff sounds true" – how do you reconcile that conflict?The answer is to listen to your Spirit, pay attention to what's true, and avoid listening to the false messages that surround us.

Connect with the wonder that you are.We've identified with the gal on the front of this book because we have falsely referred to ourselves as Wonder Woman – when the truth is, we are Wonderous Women!

So, What Is a Wonderous Woman?

- A Wonderous Woman is someone who –
- sets her own expectations,
- focuses on her priorities,
- understands her gifts,
- is grateful for her uniqueness,
- recognizes her value,
- avoids comparing herself to others,
- is clear that she doesn't have to do it "all",
- finds joy in small things,
- pursues her dreams,
- makes them a priority,
- is comfortable in her own skin, and
- realizes that her happiness can make a difference in the lives of those she loves.

We can find important truths about how God created us in the Bible.As we read them below, rejoice in the fact that God knows YOUR name.

> *"Before I formed you in the womb I knew you, and before you were born, I consecrated you."*
>
> **Jeremiah 1:5**
>
> *"So, God created man (and woman) in his own image ..."*
>
> **Genesis 1:27a**
>
> *"For we are his workmanship, created in Christ Jesus for good works, which God prepared beforehand, that we should walk in them."*
>
> **Ephesians 2:10**
>
> *"Why, even the hairs of your head are all numbered. Fear not; you are of more value than many sparrows."*
>
> **Luke 12:7**

Here are some comments that support the necessity of connecting who you are and finding the Wonderous Woman inside.

> *"A true Wonder Woman is a woman pursuing her passions and living her life the best way she knows how, even if the dishes remain in the sink overnight. A true Wonder Woman is a woman who is doing her best, no matter what that might represent. A true Wonder Woman is a woman who is at peace with herself, her goals and her path."*
>
> **Marissa S. Chicago IL**
>
> *"I repeat this incantation daily: 'I am NOT Martha Stewart!'*
>
> *'I know who I am. I am very comfortable in my skin and have long stopped wondering if I should heed the well-meaning*

advice of other parents... then I realize they aren't walking in my shoes. So, I take comfort in the words of Robert Frost's "The Road Not Taken":

"I shall be telling this with a sigh –

Somewhere ages and ages hence:

Two roads diverged in a wood, and I—

I took the one less traveled by,

And that has made all the difference."

Laurel E

– Washington DC

"My take on this Wonder Woman business...

I have learned through experience that trying to be the perfect wife and mom of 3 creates too much stress in my life and caused a breakdown.

Trying to be Wonder Woman is the perfect description of what I was trying to do!

Was it worth it? No, but it wasn't until I had a breakdown that I realized what the heck role I was trying to fulfill.

Sometimes you just have to take a step back and look at the whole picture.

In the eyes of my husband, I am still the perfect wife and mother even though dinner might not have been made that evening, or the house isn't completely dusted, or a load of laundry is still sitting on the floor to be done.

I feel that living a purpose-filled, balanced life requires certain characteristics. Here are a few:

Figure out what your purpose is in life

1. *Be happy (and happy in love!)*
2. *Have a positive mindset*
3. *Have gratitude and lots of it!*
4. *Choose only friends that have a positive mindset*

Learning (to devote time to) personal development in my life has created so many more happy times... for myself, my husband and even my children. Being happy is very contagious.

I think to keep our cape out of the vacuum cleaner, we need to take a step back and evaluate everything in our life. What can you improve on? What stresses can you eliminate in your life?

Always try to focus on the positive in everything we do and say, have gratitude, and be happy!!! Truly enjoy our lives and everyone in it, because we never know how long we're going to be here on earth."

Michelle N.

Buffalo NY

Well said, Ladies.Maybe you girls should get together and write a book!

CHAPTER 3
YOUR PASSIONS UNCOVER YOUR PURPOSE

ANGELS DANCED ON THE DAY WE WERE BORN. THEY CELEBRATED THE PERSON WE ARE AND WHO WE WERE MEANT TO BE.

We each have been given a purpose, a personal destiny for which we are to live our lives.And, when we are "on purpose" we experience joy, fulfillment and confidence. When we aren't "on purpose," things seem harder, and we sometimes may find ourselves asking "What's the point?"

The Wonder Woman Trap is seductive because of what we believe being Wonder Woman will get us.Actually, if our efforts are not aligned with our passions, the result will be exhaustion, regret, resentment, a sense of spinning our wheels, the déjà vu of doing the same kinds of things over and over, and never feeling satisfied.This is particularly frustrating when we are doing something we are good at and are always "scoring."For some, the scorecard produces a false sense of purpose.When we find ourselves in this situation, we assume that we must be doing what we were sent here to do… because "Look how good we are at it!"

Though we have these natural gifts, we may be using them in ways that don't feed our spirit and aren't critical to our living our purpose.

Before we can determine our "Passions and Purpose" we need to understand the meaning of the terms – and how the two work together in our lives.Our talents and what we need are also in play here.Let's look at the definition of each.

Steve Pavlina, a personal development coach, breaks it down in a way that we found easy to understand.

Need – What you *must* do

Talent – What you *can* do

Passion – What you *love* to do

Purpose – What you are *meant* to do

He goes on to say:

> *"Many people see these 4 areas as inherently in conflict. How many times have you heard people spout limiting beliefs such as, 'You can't make money (need) doing what you love (passion)? Nonsense.'*
>
> *I believe that everyone can find a path on which all four of these areas are in harmony. You can find a way to work from your greatest strengths, doing what you love to do, in the service of Purpose, and taking care of all your basic needs — even achieving abundance."*

Most of us are familiar with our talents and our needs.We'd like to dive a little deeper into Passion and Purpose.

Defining our Purpose

Our purpose was defined by God before we were born.It is simply who we were sent here to be.It's the real reason we are here – the reason we exist.We can recognize this by considering the things that feel most important to us.Every time we are engaged in this experience or activity we feel completely fulfilled.

So, how do we go about uncovering our Purpose?

Living one's purpose is a topic that has created quite a buzz among speakers, spiritual leaders, celebrities, and coaches.So, why is it such a hot topic?We believe that many of us feel like something is missing or we want to feel valued and know that our lives have a purpose or that we can make a difference.Understanding your "Life's Purpose" may seem overwhelming. We've found that when you are On Purpose you will experience some of these feelings:

- You're having fun
- You're motivated
- You feel energetic
- You love to serve others
- You're courageous
- You're completely in tune
- Your heart feels connected
- You find certain activities are easy to do
- You're "hearts in it"
- You feel a sense of satisfaction

You may want to spend some quiet time answering some of these questions as you consider your purpose. We've given you some space below each question to jot down your thoughts, or you may want to use your journal.

When you were a child, what did you just love to do?What were you good at?

What do you want in your life?

Who are you without your job or money?

What makes your heart sing?

What activities could you add to your life to create more joy?

____

____

____

____

If money was no object, what would you be doing?

____

____

____

____

What would you like to change in the world?

____

____

____

____

Another option is to write down what you believe your purpose to be.Write as many ideas as you can.Avoid using any filters.Then re-read your list and identify the ones that affect your emotions.These are clues to your purpose.

If you still feel stuck, try this exercise.Think of what you want folks to say about your life – the difference that you made.Write a 100th birthday speech that you'd like to have read about what you've done with your life – the difference that you've made.Give it a try – it is really helpful to solidify your thoughts about your purpose.

When we are looking at the purpose of our lives, we can get overwhelmed thinking that it has to be something spectacular and world-changing.It doesn't.We aren't living anyone else's life.We're living ours.We want to know our value and know that we've made a difference by being here.

> *"To the world, you may be just one person, but to one person you may be the world"*
>
> ***~ Brandi Snyder***

Defining Our Passions

Passions reside in your heart, not your head.If we allow our heads to take over, we may succumb to limiting beliefs and turn our efforts towards something that "makes sense."When we listen to our hearts, possibilities begin to surface – hope shows up – and we begin to dream.

Passions are dimensions of your life where – when you are engaged in them – time disappears, judgment disappears, and even hunger can disappear.Living your passion is effortless.You are completely and authentically yourself.You might be doing exhausting physical activities, sweating bullets, and be completely unaware that what you are doing is what 90% of the world would consider "work."For you, it is no work at all.

Ruth was called to encourage women over 30 years ago.She wasn't sure what that meant, but in her heart, she knew it was right.She thought of several ideas that didn't pan out at the time, so she quietly put it on the back burner, or so she thought.

Ruth and Brenda met in the staffing industry over 30 years ago.At the time, the industry attracted a lot of women employees but not in the role of management.They rose through the ranks in the organization and into senior leadership positions.Ruth quickly realized that she was able to fulfill her calling by encouraging all the women who worked with her to be the best they could be. And her heart was happy! She looked forward to going to work!

Brenda enjoyed solving problems and making everyone happy with the outcome. As she realized this was a strength, she enjoyed showing others how to create a win/win for all sides. She realized that finding solutions that benefit everyone was huge but empowering others to do the same was not only a game changer in growing the business but also in the lives of others. Her passion for mentoring others to succeed is what transforms a good business into a great one, making every day at work an opportunity for fun and growth personally as well as professionally. She loves seeing people around her "WIN"!It's so gratifying!

What makes your heart sing?Too often, we find ourselves fulfilling many roles – business leaders, wives, mothers, homemakers, caretakers, teachers, daughters, etc. It's easy to lose sight of what we are truly passionate about.Mark Twain phrased it best when he said, "Dance like no one is watching, love like you'll never be hurt, sing like no one is listening, and live like it's heaven on earth."

Ask yourself "What is my heart's desire?"Write down everything that comes to mind.Is it to spend time outdoors enjoying nature?Is it music, or spending time traveling to amazing places? Do you want to tell your story to others, share your experiences with young women, or teach a class? The old saying "If you love your work, you'll never work a day in your life!" is true.Discover your passion – then respond to it.Find avenues that will give you the chance to experience your passion. You deserve to live your passion.

Take a few minutes to write down your heart's desire below.

____

____

____

____

Another key to your passions can be found in what you don't want in your life.Notice what you passionately dislike – and then turn it around.For example: if you hate to be around certain people because they treat everyone with disrespect, then think about the opposite of that.Write the opposite down as something you do want.For example, I surround myself with people who uplift others, are confident in their purpose, and inspire me to be the same!

Be completely honest – no one's looking!Well… no one else is looking.But you, your inner self, your highest you… SHE is certainly watching.

Our Passions are clues to our Life's Purpose.This is huge.It is vitally important that we gain clarity around what they are. "The Passion Test – The Effortless Path to Discovering Your Life Purpose", sums this idea up for us with a great quote by Janet Bray Attwood, "When you are clear, what you want will show up in your life, and only to the extent that you're clear." There are a lot of experts on the subject of passion, purpose and living the life of your dreams.The best-selling book "The Secret" by Rhonda Byrne helps us identify the untapped power that is within each of us.Wayne Dyer's book, "The Power of Intention", teaches that if we change the way we look at things, the things we look at will change. These thought-leaders share a common theme – visualize yourself living the life you want.

Olympic gold medalists, before their event, close their eyes and visualize every turn, every step, and every milestone along the race.They visualize themselves crossing the finish line and receiving the gold medal.They experience the exhilaration of success.The main point here is that they visualize the outcome as if they are already living it.

Okay, it's your turn.Take a few minutes to visualize what your optimal life will look like.Here are some ideas to think about.Some of the things that might be important to you include your relationships, what you like to do for fun, where you live, things you are doing for others and the kind of work you may be doing.Once you come up with the list of things that are important to you then visualize how it feels when you are living thispassion.The reason this is critical is that you need to get in the habit of visualizing a life filled with Passion every day.

Here's some space for your notes.

____

____

____

____

____

____

You may be thinking – "Geez! I can't get everything done that I have to do now!How do I add something else?"

We don't want you to think that you have to add something else to your list of things to do.It isn't about DOING.It is about BE-ing… but before you can get there – Awareness must come.

After all, the purpose of this book is to help you find balance in the midst of it all.But we do know that to find the balance that we are looking for, we must be clear about our passions and use that knowledge to make decisions that move us closer to living a life that is full of Passion and Purpose.

Living Your Passionate Life

Our natural tendency is to look at our list and start putting an action plan together to accomplish it.We were taught how to do that in "Goal Setting 101". While that works when setting goals, living our passions isn't about the "How".Our responsibility is to be clear about our passions – the "How" will follow.

When we understand that we don't have to know the "How" it can be quite liberating.On the other hand, it can be a little scary.We were excited when we learned that our list of passions is a guide to making choices - and our job is to be open to the opportunities that arise, and then step into those opportunities.It makes sense and the burden of having to know exactly how to make everything work goes away.That in itself alleviates the need to engage our Wonder Woman superpowers.

Remember, our passions reside in our hearts.The desires of our hearts are God-given.They were planted in our hearts when we were born.And we are promised that we will be given the desires of our hearts.

A key concept that we have embraced from the book, "The Passion Test" includes three keys to consciously creating the life you want.

The first key is **Intention** – consciously stating what you choose to create in your life is the first step in manifesting it.Remember, clarity is so important here.

The next key is **Attention** – Give attention to that which you choose to create in your life, and it will begin to show up.Have you ever decided to buy a particular make and model of car and then begin to notice that it seems like everyone else drives the same? Or, if you've been pregnant, you all of a sudden notice "everyone" is pregnant.Whatever you put your attention on – will appear.

The third key is **No Tension** – letting go of the "How" ... be open to what is appearing in this moment.This is probably one of the most difficult things to do, especially those of us who are "make it happen" kinds of gals!Ruth had an experience that proved this point.

"I am a very determined person. I am action oriented, and I tend to take things into my own hands. In many instances, that has served me "well" but I now know that if I express my desire versus. solving the problem on my own, I will be given the desire of my heart in ways that I can't dream up for myself!

My daughter Ashlee had back surgery when she was in her late twenties. I went to the hospital to be with her and was in the room when the admissions clerk came in to establish Ashlee's file.When asked if her insurance paid for a private room, she said "No." She was given the cost of a private room that would be charged should she choose to go that route. She and her husband decided to save the money and accept a semi-private room.

As "Wonder Mom" I wanted to say that I would gladly pay for her to have a private room, but it really was not my place to do so. So, I considered what was so important to me about Ashlee having a private room.I realized that I wanted her to have a good rest so she could heal.So, I prayerfully asked that she have a place where she would be given great care and have the ability to rest comfortably and quietly.

After surgery, we were told that the floor on which she was scheduled to stay, was full. As a result, she was placed on the VIP floor of the hospital which was reserved for dignitaries and royalty. Her room was not only private, but it resembled a room in a five-star hotel! The room was furnished with cherry wood furniture. Her water and ice were delivered in a silver ice bucket by a man dressed as a butler. The menu was leather-bound and had entrees that you'd find in an upscale restaurant. At 3:00 p.m. high tea was served.

My imagination would have never dreamt this possible! The desire of my heart was fulfilled beyond measure!"

Brenda had a desire in her heart for years.Interestingly, she too was reminded not to worry about the "How".

"I met my husband, Joe, several years ago.When we started dating, he was living in Tampa with his children, and I was living in Houston with my daughter.For years, we managed a long-distance relationship, but it wasn't easy.Traveling back and forth between cities every other weekend was difficult, but we made it fun by having 26 mini vacations a year while our children were with their other parents.

I always had faith that we'd end up together...in the same city.Though it was my heart's desire I tried not to worry about the "How".I was the President of a national firm with the corporate headquarters in Houston.With our lives entrenched in our cities and with children to think of it just didn't seem possible.Joe said early on, "Don't worry about the 'How' – it will happen."

To my surprise, the company for which I was President was sold and my position was eliminated!Though devastated, I was then free to live and work wherever I wanted. My daughter started college the following year, so I didn't need to uproot her.

At about the same time, Joe's company was growing so fast, they needed him to relocate to their corporate office – Las Vegas.

The perfect storm became the perfect solution.This was very different than what I expected and better than I could have ever dreamt.Rather than one of us moving to the other's home, we were able to start our new lives in a totally different city.

Las Vegas became a journey that we both could share!"

The notion here is that we limit our blessings when we try to take control of the "How".Ruth would not have ever been able to pick that hospital room because she didn't even know that kind of hospital accommodation existed.If she had been "Wonder Mom" and paid for the private room, her daughter would have missed a beautiful blessing.

If Brenda had continued to be "in charge" she and Joe would have ended up living in either Tampa or Houston.They would have tried to consolidate in one place or the other and THEN Las Vegas would have appeared at additional stress and cost!

The key here is to be open to all the possibilities not just your limited beliefs of what can be.Step into opportunities that present themselves.They will show up if you are keeping your focus and attention on your passions.

Living your passions involves being aware of your choices in all aspects of your life and choosing the things that get you closer to living your passions.Because of our "nurturing genes" we women have a tendency to take care of everyone else first and then (when and if we ever have time) we'll look inside ourselves and give some thought to what our hearts are telling us to do.

We asked women around the globe to identify the importance of living a Passion-Filled Life.Here are some of their thoughts:

> *"I have to follow my passion. When I don't, I'm not running fully fueled. I have to admit I'm addicted to being the best I can for myself and others. I grow and learn when I do what I am passionate about. And, when I do what I love I have so much more to offer. It feels right and fits like a glove. What I do is 100% for me AND 100% for my clients. I like waking up excited and love receiving calls and emails about how my work has transformed others."*
>
> **Deborah Hill**
>
> **The Awareness Initiative – Atlanta GA**
>
> *"A woman who lives her passion is someone who does not sell her soul for a secondary gain but stands true and clear."*

Siv Rognstead

Oslow Area, Norway

"My passion or search for my passion has without a doubt guided my career today.I gave up the head-of-department role in secondary school some 8 years ago in search of a more fulfilling direction in life. Since then, I have established myself as an artist, property developer and manager.I now study marketing and have spent the last few years building up my marketing business.Still, something is missing, and I am still in search of my passion. Now, though, I believe that I have found the missing link - I have spent my adult life searching for some kind of fulfillment in my career and for me, it is linking my work life to doing something that will have a real impact and help where help is so desperately needed. This first project of mine is to help the orphans in Haiti, I feel drawn and passionate in my efforts - when all the cards are starting to flip over, I am fighting to flip them back.Life without passion is a life without living."

Joy R.

- Bristol, United Kingdom

When Ruth and Brenda began their careers in the staffing industry, they found that the industry fed our passion to help others in their careers.Placing them in the right positions and seeing them excel was exciting.We felt like we were making a difference.When they left the staffing industry, we found another outlet for our passions.Because they were clear about our passions and purpose, they were able to transition into helping women find theirs.The staffing business didn't define them.It was the vehicle for them to engage their passions.The passion didn't change, just the sandbox they played in.

Dr. Wayne Dyer, internationally renowned author and speaker, says "If you are what you have, and the things you have go away, then who you are goes away."

As you can see, uncovering and living your passions will result in living a more fulfilling and joyful life of purpose.If you are clear about your passions, your daily choices will align with the activities that will get you closer to living your passion.

Don't get caught up saying yes to everything – this causes you to put the Wonder Woman cape back on and do it all over again.In most instances, we won't be called upon to make significant changes in our lives – but by making daily choices in favor of our Passions we may find that we are living our Passion or at least moving closer to the most important things.

Clarifying your passions and discovering your purpose can be one of the biggest steps you take.When you start saying "no" to things that don't matter and "yes" to those that do, you'll begin to see Wonder Woman giving way to the Wonderous Woman you are.

CHAPTER 4

DARE TO DREAM BIG

Did you know that dreamers live longer? It's true. Dr. Mehmet Oz, author of *You - The Owner's Manual"* and lead heart surgeon at New York University says, "People with passion and dreams live 7 – 10 years longer than those just going through the motions". We need to reconnect to what makes us happy. If we were lucky, we had parents and teachers who encouraged dreaming. Too often though, we were told to be "realistic."

When Ruth and Brenda were young girls, they had dreaming down pat. They dreamed about who we wanted to grow up to be.They dreamed about getting married to the perfect guy.Okay, raise your hand if you ever practiced writing your first name with a guy's last name over and over on a sheet of paper!The sky was the limit! Dreaming is the gateway to our ability to be the Wonderous Woman that we were created to be.

In Chapter 3 we talked about passions. You may be wondering about the difference between your Passions and your dreams.Dreams are products of your Passions.If your Passion is to travel the world, then your dream could be that you want to spend two weeks out of every year in a villa in Majorca, Spain with someone who makes your heart sing!

Our passions are the drivers of our dreams, and our dreams are what we work towards.Just as your DNA makes you one of a kind, so do your dreams.Your authenticity when you create your dreams and then share them with the world creates a sense of joy in your spirit.Being authentic and honest with yourself is the most important thing you can do to achieve your dreams.Your dreams need to be ***your*** dreams.No one can impose upon you what *they* believe your dreams should be.And guess what?It's never too late to dream!

Brenda had a dream of being a professional, a wife, and a mother.Other people had different ideas.

"Dinner was either something quick or take-out. I couldn't wait to get home and spend time with my daughter. My entire night was all about spending quality time with my little girl - feeding her, laughing at the food all over her face as she blew more out than went in, rolling on the floor, blowing on her tummy, and playing peek-a-boo. We had so much fun together! I even have videos to remind myself of how wonderful those times were.

You see, I made sure to take advantage of every moment and felt fulfilled in every aspect of my life. For me, having it "all" meant working, having a housekeeper, and a sitter who came to my home. You never know until you ask, my employer agreed to my having off every other Friday. I used those Fridays to go to the park, the mall, and the library with my daughter. We also painted figurines together. Today, I have a cherished collection of figurines that remind me of those special times.

I was able to enjoy this schedule until my daughter started kindergarten. I was so grateful that my dream of being a professional, wife, and mother had come true. However, I was criticized for not staying home with my daughter even though we were financially able to live on one salary. It was assumed that I would be a "stay-at-home" mom, but I chose to work because it was the perfect situation for me- I needed my career to feel whole. When I arrived home in the evenings, I was able to give all of my attention to my daughter and the quality of our time spent together was just what I had hoped for.

I knew that no one could choose my dreams for me and I'm so glad that I didn't let the pressure of others change my decision."

Dreams are visionary creations of your imagination

What are your dreams?Are they fuzzy?Do they exist?Go back to Chapter 3 and look at your passions.Reading and feeling your excitement about them will trigger your imagination.Release any expectations you may have of HOW you think your dreams will come true.But with every fiber of your being, expect that they will as you busy yourself enjoying who and where you already are.

Take a few minutes now and list your dreams here:

____

____

____

____

Like your Passions, it is important to keep your dreams front and center.There are lots of ways to do this.We love these three ideas because they are creative and fun.You pick the one that resonates most with you and get started!

Create a Dream Journal

Treat yourself to a brand new, beautiful journal. Do you have a favorite pen?Use it!Close your eyes and start experiencing "living your dream."What are you doing?How does it feel?Who is with you?As you write down your dreams, be sure to use phrases like I am… or I'm with… Use your five senses to put yourself in a place where you are already achieving your dreams.For example, Ruth dreams of speaking to large groups of women at a beautiful venue by the ocean, listening to the waves off her balcony while drinking a cup of hazelnut-flavored coffee as she watches the sunrise!

Create a Vision Board

Picture yourself living your dream.Find pictures that represent each of your dreams.For example, if you dream of going to Paris, find a picture of the Eiffel Tower or another picture that represents Paris for you.Magazines are great sources for pictures.Also, consider using phrases that represent your dreams.Ruth created a vision board that included pictures of travel, speaking and a man and a woman holding hands.She then posted her vision board on her Match.com profile where she met her husband, Buck.He told Ruth later that one of the things about her profile that he appreciated was her Vision Board.He said to himself, “now that’s a woman who knows what she wants!”

Get busy and get a poster board and create a collage of all of the pictures that represent what you want in your lifeUse all of your creative juices!We like lots of glitz, so our boards usually have a few colors of glitter on them. This is a great activity to do with a friend!

Manifest Your Dreams: The Power of Intention and Action

The journey to achieving our dreams can often feel like an uphill battle, filled with obstacles and challenges that seem insurmountable. Yet, the wisdom of influential thought leaders like Deepak Chopra, Gabrielle Bernstein, and Oprah Winfrey suggests that the power of manifestation can bring us closer to realizing our aspirations. It's a concept that transcends mere wishful thinking and enters the realm of tangible action.

To some, the idea of manifestation invokes the thought of magic or relying on luck.But it’s not.It's about aligning our intentions with our actions. It's a process that begins with setting a clear intention, nurturing a strong belief in our God-given capabilities, and then taking concrete steps toward our goals. This approach combines the law of attraction with the law of action, creating a potent formula for success.

As we mentioned previously, creating a vision board is one of the most effective tools in the manifestation toolkit. It serves as a visual representation of our desires, a constant reminder of where we aim to be. By selecting images and words that resonate with our goals, we can keep our focus sharp and our spirits high.

But a vision board is more than just a collage of dreams; it's a *catalyst for change.* It encourages us to be proactive, cultivate patience, foster better relationships, to explore the world, to pursue our ideal careers, and practice self-compassion. Each image, each word, is a commitment to ourselves—a pledge to pursue the life we envision.

So, if you find yourself questioning whether your dreams are within reach, remember that manifestation is a journey of both belief and action. Set your intention, believe in your potential, and take the steps necessary to weave your dreams into the fabric of your reality. Your vision board is not just a collection of images; it's a roadmap to the future you desire.

Embrace the power of manifestation and watch as the impossible becomes possible. Your dreams are not just figments of your imagination—they are the blueprints for your future. Start building, start manifesting, and let your dreams unfold before your eyes.

Brenda is a testament to the incredible power of vision and goal setting. By creating a clear and compelling vision for her future, Brenda was able to set her intentions and align her actions toward achieving her dreams. With Joe by her side, they were able to manifest a beautiful, fully paid home and the freedom to travel extensively.

This narrative is more than just inspiring; it's a blueprint for anyone looking to realize their aspirations. It shows that when you set your intention and diligently align your actions with your goals, the universe conspires to turn your dreams into reality. Brenda's journey illustrates that with determination, commitment, and a clear vision, anything is possible.

So, what's your vision for the future? How will you align your actions to achieve your goals? Let Brenda's success story motivate you to start crafting your path to fulfillment. Dream big, set your intentions, and take action – your future is waiting for you!

Girls, get busy and get a poster board, and create a collage of all of the pictures that represent what you want in your life.Use all of your creative juices!We like lots of glitz, so our boards usually have a few colors of glitter on them. This is a great activity to do with a friend!

As we mentioned, these are our favorite ideas, but you may have an idea that works best for you.Your goal is to create a visual that you keep in front of you daily.Just as with your Passions, attention to your dreams is important.And remember as you create your dreams and see yourself living them!Leave time, money, and the "how" out of the picture!

One size does not fit all!

Daily, we are inspired by people who reach their dreams.Observing others overcome significant odds helps us believe that we too can reach our dreams.We may find ourselves both motivated and intimidated by the success that others have had.Because our dreams are as unique as our DNA, it's important to remember that everyone does not dream of scaling Mount Everest, flying a plane around the world, or creating a new vaccine.Some dreams involve spending quality time with your family or taking a vacation to Italy with your girlfriends. The point here is, to believe that your dreams are important and worthwhile, and you deserve them!

Attaining your dreams

You have taken the first steps to achieving your dreams by setting the intention and writing each one down.Because you are placing your attention on your dreams daily, you will begin to recognize opportunities that come your way that will help you fulfill your dreams. Take action when these opportunities arise even though they may be different from what you expected.Sometimes it takes courage to step into something that may look different or unusual.When you are committed to reaching your dreams, you will find the courage you need to move forward.

We also encourage you to share your dreams with people who will support you.Ruth experienced this firsthand.

"I was visiting one of our offices in Houston and noticed that Lisa Vise, one of our employees, had a picture of a car on her calendar.I hate to date myself, but this was a time in which we only used the desk calendars that flipped from one day to the next.Anyway, I asked Lisa about the picture of the car on her calendar, and she told me that it was her "dream car."I asked her why she had the picture on her calendar, and she told me that every day, she was forced to touch the picture of the car to turn the page on her calendar.It was a daily reminder that she was looking forward to owning the car.

I loved that idea!I would check with Lisa regularly to see how close she was to getting her car and delighted in being a part of her dream experience. Then, one day, she told me to step out to the driveway of our corporate offices and watch her drive into the garage with her new car! I was thrilled to see her behind the wheel of that car!

Recently, I contacted Lisa to ask her permission to use her story.We had a great exchange about the experience, and she told me "I remember so well that picture and the beautiful car.It was a Buick Rivera.I've had a few cars since then and some were even nicer than the Rivera.But I've never felt the same excitement or gotten the same pleasure out of any other car.It was very special."

Lisa was very adept at achieving her dreams.She now is one of two principal owners of her own staffing company in Houston, Texas.

I've shared this story over and over with people in my training classes because it taught me two things.The first – the value of keeping your dream in front of you, and second – the value of sharing your dream with others who will support you!"

When you find your voice and speak your dream with clarity and focus, you tap into your power. It's the power to move people, to create a collective force that is indeed unstoppable.

So, how do you become this visionary? It starts with self-reflection. Understand what drives you, what your core values are, and what you want to achieve. Then, refine your dream until it's crystal clear. Next, share it passionately, with every ounce of conviction you have. And finally, connect with those who resonate with your vision, those who see what you see and are eager to help make it a reality.

Remember, the journey of a visionary is not a solo flight. It's a voyage that thrives on collaboration, mutual respect, and shared aspirations. So, find your tribe, speak your truth, and watch as the world aligns with your dream. Together, there's no limit to what you can achieve. Dream big, speak boldly, and let your vision soar.

> *Ruth and Brenda both had a love for the staffing industry, even though they had different styles and took different paths within the industry. They shared a common passion: they loved seeing people grow and enjoyed mentoring them to reach their full potential. Witnessing people achieve their goals brought immense joy, which is why they loved their jobs. Finding the Passion in what you do is key.*

Attaining your dreams is a choice. You may find yourself thinking "when this happens, I'll be able to..." or, "I don't have time for me right now, I have to…"This thinking will delay the joy of reaching your dreams.Have you ever watched someone rise to celebrity status seemingly overnight?Chances are there were a lot of choices that were made along the way that got him/her to that point.

Let's talk about taking action towards our dreams. We all have them, but sometimes we let our fears and excuses get in the way. It's time to change that. Here are some constructive ideas to help you get started:

- Recognize that your dreams are important and worth pursuing.
- Believe in yourself and your ability to make your dreams a reality.
- Don't let anyone or anything hold you back from pursuing your dreams.
- Set achievable goals and take small steps towards them every day.
- Be kind to yourself and focus on positive self-talk.
- Take care of your physical and mental health so you have the energy and focus to pursue your dreams.
- Learning is a lifelong process. Keep growing and expanding your knowledge and skills.
- Remember that every day is a new opportunity to work towards your dreams. With these constructive ideas, you can start taking action toward your dreams. Don't let your fears and excuses hold you back any longer. You got this!

If she can do it, so can I!

There are so many beautiful stories of women who have reached their dreams.As we looked at the stories that we wanted to share with you, these themes came to mind.The first supports the value of writing down your dreams and holding them close to your heart.And the second speaks to believing in your gifts and dreams regardless of how others may react.

Oprah Winfrey introduced Tererai Trent to us on national television.As a young girl in rural Zimbabwe, Tererai lived without running water and electricity and had no hope for her future. She remembers the day that her father said that the boys in her village were the future and needed education and the girls would be married.Tererai was desperate to learn so she secretly did her brother's homework.

The boy's teacher learned of Tererai's secret and asked that she be allowed to go to school.She was able to attend school for two terms, but she was forced to get married at the age of 11.She had three children by the time she was 18.Her husband beat her when he realized she wanted to have an education.

Jo Luck, from Heifer International, visited Tererai's village and asked every woman about her greatest dream.Some of the women didn't even know they were allowed to have dreams.But Tererai said that she wanted to go to America, get her BS degree, followed by a master's degree, and then her PhD.By all standards, the odds of her achieving these goals would seem insurmountable.But Jo told Tererai that if she truly desired her education, it would be achievable.

Another amazing woman in Tererai's life was her mother.She encouraged Tererai to write her dreams on a piece of paper.Tererai wrote them down, put them in a scrap of tin and buried them under a rock in a pasture.Tererai wrote "As a woman without an education, life will continue to be a burden.I truly believe in these dreams, and I hope one day to work for the causes of women and girls in poverty.

In 1998, Tererai moved to Oklahoma with her husband and now five children.Three years later, she earned her bachelor's degree in agriculture education.She earned her master's degree in 2003, the same year her husband was deported for abuse.

Tererai returned home after earning each degree, retrieved the tin filled with her dreams and checked off each one she accomplished.In 2009, Tererai realized her greatest dream – her Ph.D.

Tererai is a symbol of hope in her village.She returned to her village and along with her mother, gave the girls pens, paper, and tiny metal tins.They are encouraging a new generation to dream.

Recently, we read an article in the Washington Post about Suzanne Watson who realized her dream to become a doctor at age 57.She applied for medical school as a young woman. She was accepted and she began taking classes married, with a 9-month-old baby.After learning that she was pregnant again, she decided to quit medical school.

She and her husband settled down, and she felt a calling to become an Episcopal priest. She was able to work part-time, which really suited her life as a wife and mother. Right after she was ordained, her husband committed suicide.He just couldn't deal with the stigma of mental illness.

When someone commits suicide, insurance companies don't typically pay life insurance benefits as it was in Suzanne's case. So, she sold her house, moved into a smaller one, the children changed schools, and she began working full-time in her role as a priest.

But she had never lost the dream of practicing medicine. When she was 50, she started to take stock of the years she had left, and her son said to her, "You know, I've heard you talk about this your entire life, and you either need to do it now and sign up tomorrow, or you need to just shut up about it." And she decided to give med school another chance.

At the time of the article, she was in her second year as a resident! There are so many wonderful stories of lives being changed as a result of following one's dreams. Feed your spirit with inspiration.In this wonderful age of the Internet, we can put our hands on a treasure chest of stories like these.

Your dream is necessary, not only for you but to bring the change all of us desire.

Many of you reading this book have your own stories.If you feel led to share your story, or, if you'd like to share your dreams with Ruth and Brenda the address is:

info@ruthwheatauthorspeaker.com

Step out there; know that you can dream big.One of our favorite sayings is “thoughts become things.” Think about it.Everything around you was someone’s idea - knee-high pantyhose, spanks, cleavage coolers - all developed by someone who had an idea!Personally, except for the way spanks feel, we’re very grateful for these inventions!

Here’s a great poem about dreaming, if you still need a little encouragement.

Be What You Want to Be!

There is inside you

all of the potential

to be whatever you want to be,

all of the energy

to do whatever you want to do.

Imagine yourself as you would like to be,

doing what you want to do,

and each day, take one step

towards your dream.

And though at times it may seem too

difficult to continue,

hold on to your dream.

One morning you will awake to find

that you are the person you dreamed of,

doing what you wanted to do,

simply because you had the courage

to believe in your potential

and to hold on to your dream.

Author Unknown

CHAPTER 5

ROADBLOCKS TO LIVING OUR PASSIONS AND ACHIEVING OUR DREAMS

If it was "easy" everyone on the planet would be living their passions and achieving their dreams.Picture this:you are wearing your Wonder Woman Cape, and it is stuck in the vacuum.Every time you take a couple of steps forward, the vacuum pulls you back.The vacuum represents fear and limiting beliefs that keep us from living the lives we want.

There are two types of people - Those who can't get traction to accomplish what they want and simply give up; and those who figure out a way to get their cape out of the vacuum and succeed.

Our experience tells us that fear is the number one way that we sabotage our dreams.

When we take a look at Fear, we realize that it is an emotional response to something we *think* will happen.Sometimes those perceptions are based upon evidence and other times they are based upon someone else's belief system that we unknowingly take on as our own.

In this chapter, we examine three Fears – two of which you may be very familiar with.One may surprise you, but it is very real.

Fear of Failure

The fear of failure has convinced us that it is much better to avoid the pain of going for something and not achieving it.It is one of the greatest fears people have.Successful people overcome the fear of failure and unsuccessful people do not.The "agony of defeat" can be crippling.However, you have a choice.You can choose to allow failure to keep you from trying again or you can choose to learn from the experience, make some adjustments and go for it!

A reporter asked Thomas Edison about the thousands of experiments that he went through to invent the carbon filament used in light bulbs.He said something along the lines of, "How does it feel to have failed 10,000 times before you created the carbon filament?"Thomas Edison replied, "I have not failed once.I now know definitively over 9,000 ways that an electric light bulb will not work."

On a personal note, Ruth's housekeeper Eva, had her way of dealing with the vacuum.

"Eva was vacuuming one day; one of her favorite chores, thank God! All of a sudden, the vacuum stopped working and started making a terrible sound.She tried turning it off and on again and nothing happened.She and the vacuum were stuck.

She had a couple of options at that point.She could tell me that the vacuum was broken and go home for the day, or she could fix it. The vacuum cleaner was an expensive model; guess I thought it would have better suction!Anyway, Eva could have been afraid to try to fix it herself, but she went ahead.

Now Eva is very resourceful.I found her outside with the vacuum (which by the way weighed more thanshe did) turned upside down and she was attacking the underside with a coat hanger.I'm not sure what she said, because it was in Spanish, but it appeared she was encouraging that coat hanger to solve the problem!She succeeded and finished her job beautifully.

Eva's determination made an impression on me.She didn't give up – she had something that she wanted to do, and she made it happen!"

We guess that if you look back over your life, there are times that you experienced failure and you kept going.Perhaps you had supportive family and friends who encouraged you to choose to pick up and move forward.Regardless, you can call upon that experience and relate it to the fear of failing that you may be experiencing today as you reach for your dreams.

Fear of Judgement

The second fear, rejection, relates to being told "No," and the disapproval of your choices or actions by other people.The word "no" only contains two letters, but it can have a powerful punch if we let it.Let's face it, "no" is one of the first words we're taught as toddlers.While well-intentioned, the word stopped us from doing something that we wanted to do!However, in most cases, we were being stopped from doing something that would harm us.There was no judgment about us at all!If we can remove the judgment that we impose upon ourselves when we are told "no," then the word and our experience would become a lot easier.

The word "no" may not cause you any indigestion.But the fear of judgment and disapproval of others may give you pause.Remember Brenda's story in the previous chapter?If she had given in to the fear of judgment by the people she valued, she would not have achieved the dreams she wanted for her life.

> *"Not only do I have a beautiful, self-confident daughter, but I also achieved my dream to become the first woman president of the company I worked for."*

Fear of Success

Now this one may surprise you.We've met thousands of people in our lives and they each thought they wanted to feel successful.Granted, success should be measured by our standards, but regardless of the definition of success, we want to be good at something and make a difference.We want to believe that we were created to do something special with our lives.So, how does the fear of success impact our ability to live our passions and achieve our dreams?

If we took a few minutes, we could all find areas in our lives where we have experienced the fear of changes that may take place when we reach the levels of success we want.Perhaps this fear surfaced when you were asked to take a job with a lot more responsibility or step into a situation that was exciting but very unfamiliar with a lot of unknowns.

Marianne Williamson, international lecturer, and author of best-selling books including, *The Age of Miracles, Return to Love*, and *Everyday Grace* had this to say about the fear of success.

"Our deepest fear is not that we are inadequate. Our deepest fear is that we are powerful beyond measure. It is our light, not our darkness that most frightens us. We ask ourselves, 'Who am I to be brilliant, gorgeous, talented, fabulous?' Actually, who are you not to be? You are a child of God. You're playing small does not serve the world. There is nothing enlightened about shrinking so that other people won't feel insecure around you. We are all meant to shine, as children do.

We were born to make manifest the glory of God that is within us. It's not just in some of us; it's in everyone. And as we let our light shine, we unconsciously permit other people to do the same. As we are liberated from our own fear, our presence automatically liberates others."

Unpacking Our Fears

In his article, titled "What's Holding You Back from Reaching Your Dreams," Thomas Hughes, a coach, educator, and speaker, gives us an interesting perspective on fear.

"Most fear is self-created. You simply cannot reach out and touch those fears. Yet they can be so strong that they can stop us dead in our

tracks, afraid to pursue our dreams. These fears are based upon the mental pictures (programming pictures) we have of ourselves. And they are carried with us everywhere we go."

These mental pictures often create limiting beliefs that we accept as truths about ourselves.We spent some time thinking about some of our own limiting beliefs and some that we've heard from a lot of other women.

Here's the list we came up with:

- I'm too young.
- I'm too old.
- I don't have the experience.
- I don't have the credentials.
- Others have tried and failed.
- I don't have the time.
- If I don't do this…it won't get done.
- If I do succeed, my whole life will change – it's easier to live with the status quo.
- I have to give up things I love to do this.
- I need to lose weight.
- The rules say…
- I don't have enough money.
- Thinking small.
- I could never do that (something happened that caused you to doubt yourself).

After we created this list, we began looking for women who had not let limiting beliefs stand in the way of their dreams.There are so many amazing stories out there, but these two stood out.

Dara Torres captured the hearts and minds of Americans of all ages when she launched her Olympic comeback as a new mother at the age of forty-one years after she had retired from competitive swimming and eight years after her last Olympics. We learned that the average age of an Olympian is 27, so she was definitely an anomaly.She did not let her age keep her from competing and winning in a sport that she loved. By the way, did you catch that she was also a *new mother* at the age of 41?While a lot more common today, that's still quite a feat!

Dara believes that "age is just a number."She states, "I've wanted to win at everything, every day since I was a kid.And time doesn't change a person; it just helps you get a handle on who you are.Even at age 41, I still hate losing—I'm just more gracious about it.I'm also aware that setbacks have an upside: they fuel new dreams."

Dara Torres has certainly attained world celebrity status.As a result, we have had the opportunity to learn about her amazing story. But she wasn't always a worldwide celebrity.She came from humble roots and had a dream.

Our next "rock star" is Andrea Kulberg.Her story is one of courage to overcome a challenge that life had given her, to pursue and achieve her dream.

Andrea's own life started with real adversity.Andrea was born an identical twin. By the time she was only a day old, she had already had her last rights read to her by the priest.It just was not realistic to expect a two-pound preemie to live.But at 24 hours old, Andrea's obstacles had only just begun to mount.

A nurse came in to bathe her. During that bath, Andrea turned blue because her lungs were still incapable of functioning correctly outside the incubator.Since she could not breathe, her tiny body was placed back into the incubator and the nurse turned her oxygen on the highest setting.With no one noticing her chart, or oxygen settings that were much too high, 18 days later, Andrea was blind in her right eye and was left with only extremely limited vision in her left eye.

Andrea has a condition called Retinopathy of Prematurity (ROP).There is no cure for ROP, as the retina and often the optic nerve are permanently scarred.Even after multiple surgeries, painful childhood eye drops, and countless doctor visits, Andrea remains legally blind today.

She goes about her daily life with giant prints on her computer screens.Her nose literally must touch the paper when she reads to make the words out. She cannot control her floating eye. She cannot drive.

Andrea lost her sight as a baby, but she never lost her vision.Her vision to be a rock star has been more than realized.

Despite her lack of eyesight, Andrea overcame unbelievable obstacles even as a young child.

At seven years old, rock star Andrea decided she would participate with her twin sister, Aly, in what should be known as the last sport a blind kid should ever attempt - competitive baton twirling.That's right, a sport with a spinning metal projectile flying directly in the path of your teeth, and this brave blind kid said, "Why not?"

This was not the kind of baton twirling that most people think of when they imagine a figure-eight or two in the parade.This was the kind of twirling where the baton goes flying; the twirler turns around six times, and then catches it behind her head while upside down.It was dangerous and tedious learning for any sighted child, but almost impossible for a legally blind child.

From seven years old until Andrea was about ten years old, she and her twin sister practiced baton twirling almost four hours a day, seven days a week, except when they traveled across the country to compete.

By the end of their twirling careers they had accumulated over 600 trophies, more than 1,500 medals, and a couple of World Championships. But Aly could see the baton!Andrea couldn't!Andrea knew she had the gift of timing and truly believed she could do it when everyone else thought it was impossible.

Andrea's story gives us chills every time we read it!Though some would consider her abilities to be extremely limited, she doesn't.A quote by John Wayne exemplifies how courage can make a difference in our ability to push past fear: *"Courage is being scared to death but saddling up anyway."*

We all have Wonder Woman inside us, and we can become our own heroes.The first step is recognizing what is keeping us from getting what we want.When we give these roadblocks and obstacles names, then we know what we are dealing with, and we look for specific ways to move past them.

We all experience obstacles in our lives.What are yours?How can you find a way to push past your obstacles and become your own superhero?

Obstacles I face

____

____

____

CHAPTER 6

MY WONDER WOMAN CAPE IS WRECKING MY BALANCE!

We asked women around the country to share their definitions of the Wonder Woman persona.

Boy!Can we relate to this response!

"Yes, there is the guilt (mine more so for not spending enough time with my children), but what I never expected was the effect the Wonder Woman persona had on others. You look and act as if you have everything under control, and to the outside world, you are doing a heck of a job. Inside, you know you need help, but can't ask for help, because that spoils the persona (and admit that you do not have superpowers). But no one will offer that desperately needed help either because you look and act as if you have it all under control (doing a "heck of a job") - why would you need any help???

I found this especially true when I was trying to run my solo law practice out of my house while staying home with my new baby (who is now 9). Not only did my Wonder Woman cape get stuck in the vacuum, but in the printer, in the diaper genie and I think it may have even caught fire at the stove!"

Lisa S. Barnstable
- Yarmouth, Massachusetts

Whew!We become exhausted and overwhelmed just reading this story!We've all had days just like this!Amazingly, we all pulled through – maybe a little ragged, but we pulled through.But do we just 'want to pull through' – is that enough?

Many of these pressures are put upon ourselves to what we think society expects from us. We always feel that we are not doing enough. Brenda has noticed some of these indicator's surface in her life from time to time.

"When I was a single mom, I was juggling a job as the President of a $300 million national company, walking the dog, chasing the birds away from attacking my cat, running my very social daughter to swim practice and meets, managing her very busy social calendar, and trying to find time for myself.(By the way, have you ever spent hours inhaling chlorine from an indoor pool?Let me tell you, that can give you a crazy kind of 'high!')

Even though I was happy, I felt overburdened from time to time with life and all of the activities in it.No matter how much I did, I felt like I should be doing more. Instead of being proud of the fact that I cooked dinner three nights a week, I felt guilty that it wasn't five.Many times, this juggling and feeling like you can never be enough, can bring on depression and anxiety.

This question created an interest on our part in finding out more about the number of people who might be struggling with depression.We ran across some surveys that are a little daunting.

A National Health Institute survey from 2023 indicates that 280 million people suffer from depression in the United States. There were 86 million antidepressant items prescribed in 2022/23, to an estimated 8.6 million identified patients.

Prescription drug use in the United States has reached record levels, reaching 6.3 billion prescriptions—approximately 19 prescriptions for every American— filled in 2020 alone.

Wow!There are a lot of folks who suffer from depression that are seeking professional help.And these statistics don't take into account the vast sea of the rest of us who face challenges that get us down and move us toward depression with NO help!In many cases, depression is a clinical condition but much of the time, it is a reaction to circumstance.Clinical depression should and must be addressed with the help of professionals.But for most of us, becoming depressed can be a natural consequence of the *reaction* to the lives that we lead.

These statistics are alarming and prompted us to look at some warning signs of depression.Dr. Gregory Jantz, Founder and Executive Director of The Center for Counseling and Health Resources lists 30 indicators (areas that signal caution) for depression.

Out of those 30, three jumped off the page:

- A sense of being wound up or weighed down.
- A sense of being overburdened with life and its activities.
- A lack of spiritual peace or well-being.

These three resonated with us, specifically, because of the feedback we get from people who are seeking some kind of balance in their lives.

For Ruth, these and other indicators propelled her into a deep depression.

"As I look back at that time in my life, I remember how hard I worked to appear as if everything was wonderful in my life, while on the inside I felt despair and hopelessness.Exhaustion was part of my daily existence as I struggled to portray the happy, Wonder Woman persona while living a very challenging reality.I was able to fool a lot of people, but those closest to me could tell I was struggling.One of my dear friends told me she knew something was up with me because the light in my eyes had

gone out.I guess there's a lot of wisdom in the quote that says, 'your eyes are the windows to your soul.'

Fortunately, I was diagnosed with clinical depression right away and I was able to get the help I needed to get healthy again.

My experience has led me to live authentically regardless of my personal circumstances.Living truthfully and learning how to let go of the beliefs I held about being perfect in everything, really has made a difference in my life balance."

So, how can we achieve better mental health? Embracing gratitude can significantly enhance your mental well-being. Studies have shown that gratitude can lead to a more optimistic outlook on life, increased happiness, and even a reduction in symptoms of depression and anxiety. By acknowledging the good in your life, you can shift focus from negative thoughts to positive experiences, fostering a sense of joy and contentment.

Gratitude isn't just a feeling; it's a practice that, when incorporated into daily life, can help you develop a more resilient and positive mental state. So, why not start today by reflecting on the things you're thankful for? It might just be the game-changer for your mental health needs. Here are some ways to get started!

- Get yourself a beautiful journal and write down 2 or 3 things for which you are grateful each day.Creating this gratitude journal will only take a few minutes but will positively impact your day! (Check out the "Wonderous Woman Journal" on Amazon!)
- Share your gratitude journal entries with others.How about sending a text to a family member or friend that lists what you're grateful for?Encourage them to do the same. This daily practice can have a positive effect on your day-to-day activities, and it deepens relationships.

- Set aside a "No-complain" day.Wow!This might be quite an undertaking! What a difference this can make in how you go through your day.It will have a positive effect on your spirit.

Here is some space for you to get started on your gratitude practice.Jot down a minimum of 3 things you're grateful for.

I'm grateful for...

____

____

____

____

Let's consider life balance.We believe that finding that place of balance within each of us is so important and in some cases life-preserving.That's why we wrote this book.In the next pages, we'll be sharing our thoughts about finding balance by getting to your personal core, the real person you are inside.

One of the most interesting responses we received when we posted a question regarding the Wonder Woman persona was this:

> *"I think that the Wonder Woman Phenomenon is one of the most damaging concepts to the AmericanModern woman that has come along... that somehow doing things in accordance to 'Super Human' strength is the norm now and falling below that level of production is frowned upon as weakness, inability to perform, or somehow acquiescing to a male-dominated society. Women who 'Do It All' are Wonder Women, but women who have chosen to do fewer things, but to do them with all of their heart, are somehow lesser.*

> *"How many times do we hear men comparing themselves to Flash Gordon or Spiderman? I remember NEVER, but then again, I may have been running the sweeper, answering emails, and braiding my daughter's hair and not be able to hear it... lol ... The only things I like about Wonder Woman are her FABULOUS gold cuff bracelets... the rest of the pressure she can keep for herself! "*
>
> ***Jennifer K of Sharon, PA***

Few roles are as challenging and rewarding as that of a stay-at-home mom. It's a testament to the strength and dedication of those who take on this role that they deserve a medal for their hard work.

Stay-at-home moms wear many hats and juggle numerous responsibilities daily. From being the 'Chief Home Officer' to the 'Director of Household Operations,' these titles reflect the diverse and dynamic roles they play. Some moms might prefer the humor in titles like 'Domestic Goddess' or 'Chaos Coordinator,' adding a touch of levity to the hard work they do. These titles capture the essence of the dedication and love poured into the role of a stay-at-home mom.

Now THAT is a woman for you. Only we can set standards SO HIGH that they are impossible to attain, then we diminish ourselves for not being able to perform at standards we created out of our reach.

And to that, we say a hearty, "Amen, Sister!

CHAPTER 7

BALANCE FROM THE INSIDE OUT

Mary Henton of Columbus, Ohio had this to say about the Wonder Woman persona.

"My characterization of the Wonder Woman persona? Your basic 'downer'.

In my earlier years (during active motherhood, raising children, maintaining and cultivating a career, surviving a marriage falling apart, starting a new marriage, etc.), I allowed the Wonder Woman myth to set my goal. Big mistake. Only a few little life crises, depression, growing up (well at least growing older!), and wiser women around me helped me to begin to redefine expectations – MY expectations. Hey, I'm not perfect. Still have plenty to learn here in my 50's, but I'm soaring under my own cape these days!"

Way to go, Mary!Our research has shown us that the definition of Life Balance is to put "equal emphasis" on everything that is important in our lives.Specifically, we learned to examine these categories work, family, social, spiritual, leisure, financial, and personal and make adjustments in each area to ensure "proper balance."We left this research feeling that to be balanced we had to spend the same percentage of our time in every category.At face value, we just don't see how this is possible.

We believe that Life Balance is not “one size fits all.”While the experts are right about focusing on the things that are most important to us, our priorities can and must shift based on where we are in our lives.For example, when our children are young, we spend a disproportionate amount of time caring for them versus when they leave the nest.

Finding balance should be a daily or at least weekly activity and is different for each of us.Balance comes from our core, our soul.This is when we feel that everything is right. We are living in the moment, we know where we are, who we are with, and what we are doing is perfect.

This is a very important distinction because truth exists at our very core.The exhaustion that we experience when we feel out of whack is based on living the persona that we believe everyone expects and not listening to “OUR TRUTH”.

The Lasso of Truth is Wonder Woman’s primary tool.The lasso varies in length based on the individual’s needs.It is indestructible, can restore lost memories, dispels illusions and protects from the attacks of others.The lasso can be both an offensive and defensive tool.

“Our Truth” can be used both intentionally and protectively.When we know at our core what we value, that truth can be our tool against the pressures we place on ourselves to be all things to all people.

Sometimes it’s hard to get to the “real” truth.For some of us, we may want to tell the truth that supports someone else’s plan for our lives.For some reason, we think they must know more about what we need than we do.And we fear being criticized.When we recognize that their truth about us is not ours, then we are capable of moving toward our truth.

So, if the truth is where our balance lies, our first step is to get crystal clear about that truth.Until we do, we can’t benefit from the freedom we feel when we are living our Truth.Getting clear about this truth can then be used as a barometer for achieving balance.

Searching for Truth and Finding Our Vulnerabilities

Just like superheroes, we all have areas in our lives where we are vulnerable.

Wonder Woman's friend, Superman, knows that Kryptonite will kill him.He takes measures to protect himself by avoiding kryptonite.Wonder Woman's vulnerability is not easily defined as one thing.She has multiple vulnerabilities!Amazing – Wonder Woman can even multi-task her vulnerabilities!Her most vulnerable areas include:

- **Her Build** – Wonder Woman's height and weight are similar to those of her superhero male counterparts.Her large size keeps her from being as agile as someone with a smaller frame.Even Wonder Woman had a problem with her size!How often do we find ourselves worrying about our appearance – our size?
- **Energy Vulnerability** – When caught off guard, Wonder Woman is vulnerable to high-energy attacks.Though her strength, durability, and speed are resources against freezing and fire attacks, high energy gets the best of her.We often find ourselves in the same boat.Certain areas of life sap our energy and make us vulnerable.Ever have people in your life that seem to suck the life out of you when you have a ten-minute conversation with them?When you see their number on caller ID, a little voice inside is saying, "Run, Forrest Run!" (If you're one of our friends, we are not talking about you!)
- **Piercing Weapon Vulnerability** – Wonder Woman can deflect many different types of weapons.But she's not invulnerable; she can be pierced by a high-powered rifle or advanced machine gun fire.We all have circumstances that we dodge easily.There is often that one thing, however, that can knock us off our feet and cause us to feel unbalanced.The important note here is that this "point of vulnerability" is different for every person.So, we should avoid comparing

ourselves to another's ability to weather every storm.Everyone has something in their lives that makes them vulnerable.

- **Too Compassionate** – Wonder Woman has put her own life in danger on occasion when she exhibits too much compassion.Those of us, who often find ourselves being very compassionate for others, may tend to put everyone else's needs ahead of our own.We think the airlines have figured it out.Prior to takeoff, a flight attendant reminds us to put the oxygen mask on ourselves first, so that we can then take care of others.

When we put on the Wonder Woman Cape, we completely ignore the fact that we have any vulnerability.But knowing our vulnerabilities is a very important component of the life balance puzzle.

Here's an example of how we can find ourselves entangled in a lot of activities that seem to overshadow our truth.Consider the mother of three who struggles to find quality time to spend with her children.She's called upon to volunteer at every fundraiser and event. She bakes cookies, buys the teachers gifts, and organizes the carpool.Reactively, she can cave to the pressure and agree to sign up every time she's asked. This may fuel her need to be supermom and feel appreciated.In doing so, she is constantly stressed and finds very little balance in her life.Her life is being dictated because she has chosen to meet someone else's expectations and demands. And ironically, she may find that in all of this activity, she doesn't have quality time for her children!

The intentional approach to finding balance in this instance may be to say, "No, thank you." to some or all of those requests.In doing so she is aligning her time with her priority – spending time with her children.

Being present is a gift that we all can give to ourselves and others. Getting a cell phone was such an exciting experience!We could talk to people we care about, organize our day, order our dinner whenever and wherever we wanted!Though extremely handy, our phones can become a burden that we carry around with us wherever we go. They dictate our day and steal our attention from the people around us.

One of the healthiest things we can do for ourselves is to take a break from our phones and be an example to our children and spouses to do the same. We need to show them that we care about their thoughts and feelings and that they are important to us. One way to do this is by having everyone put their phones in a basket or bowl during dinnertime. This will allow us to be fully present with our loved ones and engage in meaningful conversations.

We need to teach our children how to communicate effectively and make others feel special, no matter their age. Unfortunately, it's common to see couples and families at restaurants all staring at their phones instead of interacting with one another. We need to take back our friendships and relationships and give the gift of our presence.

Let's put away our phones for a 30-minute meal and show our loved ones how much they matter to us. Once we see faces light up when we are truly engaged, we may take further steps in our lives to be sure we are giving the gift of our full attention – it is priceless.

Just like Wonder Woman, we have to choose our battles, the ones that are important to us.Finding our truth and staying committed to that truth is our means to finding balance.

CHAPTER 8
ACHIEVING BALANCE

Some find getting to their truth easy, while others may struggle a little.Our heads tend to get in the way of our hearts. Our jobs, families, social activities – all place demands on us.

Our heads tell us that we have responsibilities that must be met.Our hearts may say "Follow your passions." The one thing we know for sure is that we must invest the time we need to get to the truth of what balance means.

Take time to listen to your heart, consider what you are passionate about, and think about your goals and dreams.Really listen, get down to your core.Once you're there, the clarity will surface, and opportunities will appear.By stepping into these opportunities, you experience joy because you are doing what is important to you.

Once you uncover the truth and are honest with yourself, the things you ***can do*** versus the things you feel you ***should do*** will surface.

It's important to stay true to that truth. We are bombarded daily with all kinds of stress.It's important to avoid becoming consumed with one big issue in your life. Sometimes situations can arise that just seem insurmountable.It's okay to focus temporarily on that problem but make every effort to include other things that are important as well.One situation that comes to mind is that of being the caregiver of someone who is ill.We can find ourselves giving all we have to give to that situation and end up with very little left for ourselves.While this is such an important endeavor, we need to find ways to meet our own needs.

We promised that we'd offer a secret to achieving balance.We're all looking for that magic bullet that will do the trick; that one thing that will make life easier and our wash whiter and brighter!While this information is not necessarily earth-shattering, it is one of *the most powerful* ways to take care of yourself and your time.Here goes –

Learn how to say "No"

The day that we realized that "No," is a complete sentence and that it doesn't require any explanation was one of the most liberating experiences we have ever had!Think about it – when we are asked to do something and we have the gumption to say "No," we feel like we owe the person requesting our time an explanation.Now, why is that?

It's important to honor your feelings and boundaries. Saying 'no' can be an act of self-care and honesty, and it allows others the opportunity to find someone who shares their enthusiasm. It's okay to prioritize your happiness and to admit that you can't be everything for everyone. By being truthful with yourself and others, you create space for more genuine experiences and prevent feelings of resentment and burnout. Remember, it's not selfish to take care of your own needs; it's necessary. When we look at the "whys" behind our compulsion to explain, we notice that we each have underlying stories that we've created about always being ready and able to serve.

Brenda was always the go-to person for everyone in her life. If someone needed help moving, she was there. If someone needed a ride to the airport, she was there. If someone needed someone to talk to, she was there. Brenda took pride in being reliable and dependable, but sometimes it came at a cost. She often felt guilty when she didn't have the time or energy to help someone. Saying "no" was difficult for her because she didn't want to let anyone down. Even if she didn't want to do the task at hand, she would agree to it out of guilt.

However, this often led to her not doing her best. She realized that it was important to be honest with herself about whether she wanted to do something or not. If she didn't have a passion for the task, it would have been better for someone else to do it. It would be better for everyone involved if the person doing the task was enthusiastic about it. For example, Brenda loved spending time with her friend Ruth. However, if Ruth suggested something that Brenda wasn't interested in, like going to a boat show, she would feel obligated to say yes.

She would dread the event and not enjoy herself. If she had said no, Ruth could have found someone who enjoyed boating to go with her. Brenda learned that it was okay to say no and that it was better to be truthful about her feelings. It allowed her to focus on the things that she was passionate about. She knew that if she said yes to everything, she wouldn't be able to give her all to anything. And, as a result, she would feel guilty about not doing her best.

Though Ruth shares some of these fears, her story involves a couple of others.

When thinking about why I have trouble saying 'No,' I realize that I need to be needed.I'm afraid of letting someone down and hate to miss out on things, even if those things require much more time than I have to allot to them. I never want to hurt someone's feelings.Sometimes I feel like if I say "No," without a good explanation the person requesting my time may feel like I don't value them.

Here's something paradoxical.Most of our careers were spent in the staffing industry.We were both very successful in sales and found ourselves coaching other young salespeople.We found that many people fear rejection, so it keeps them from picking up the phone or making a personal sales call.

For years we taught people that it is okay to hear the word "no."We remember specifically asking this question, "What is the worst thing that can happen if you make a call and the prospect says, 'No?' Can the word no really hurt you? Of course, it can't!" So, why then do we, sales trainers extraordinaire, have such a tough time saying it?

Our compulsion to say "yes," instead of "no," comes from the stories we tell ourselves, those "internal rules" that playback in our heads. Where does all of this stuff come from?Years of conditioning, experience, observation, fear, and even our value system drive us to create these stories.Somewhere along the line, the notion of saying "no" (for those of us who have trouble saying "no") was followed by some consequence that created this judgment in us.

So, what do we do about this?How do we learn how to overcome these stories that have defined us?First of all, we need to examine our stories behind saying "No," with a thoughtful eye. Then, we can ask ourselves, "Is this true, or do I believe it to be true?"

For example, let's examine Brenda's concern about letting people down when she says, "No." Is it true that Ruth would have had her feelings hurt or felt let down if Brenda had said, "No thank you, I'm not really into boat shows"?The reality is Ruth would not have felt bad and would have immediately invited someone else… and would have been grateful that she hadn't dragged her friend to an event she didn't enjoy!

To stay on track, learn how to say "no".Let go of the stories that keep you hostage.Treat your time as you would treat any other priceless asset and watch the changes a simple two-letter word can make in your life.

Remember, "No" can be a complete sentence.It's not necessary to give an explanation.Until you learn to say "No" politely, firmly and often, you'll find your calendar clogged with time-consuming commitments that can bog you down and make you feel stressed.

Support is another component of achieving balance.We mentioned earlier that when you know your truth, you begin to recognize your limits.Realizing that you have limits can be a huge step in gaining support in the areas of your life where you need it.

Support can appear in different ways.For some, emotional support is needed, and for others, it may take the form of something physical such as getting help with housework or delegating a project to someone else.Once you have that support, it helps you focus on the areas that resonate with who you are and what is truly important to you.

We work on achieving balance as if it is one big goal.As with any goal, we can work towards it each day.Balance on any given day can be defined as accomplishment, gratitude and enjoyment.Appreciate every accomplishment; relish every win - no matter how big or small.

Express gratitude for each little win during the day and keep your mind focused on the positives, leaving no room for negative thoughts.At the end of the day, when we reflect on the things we accomplished, the gratitude we experienced and the enjoyment we felt during the day, we can feel balanced that day.

Jim Bird, the founder of WorkLifeBalance.com, describes his personal life balance this way:

- Life balance is inner peace and happiness.
- Life balance is the understanding that my life is full and yet I have plenty of room to bring something new into it.
- Life balance is a happy family that I have and smiles on the faces of my girls.
- Life balance is taking care of my body without forgetting my soul.
- Life balance is walking outside and seeing the beauty around me that inspires me day after day.
- Life balance is faith that I have.
- Life balance is knowing that I do not live on the edge and that I feel secure walking through my life.

Mr. Bird finishes this list by saying:

> *"This is what Life Balance is for me.It is not some mathematical equation that I must follow in life.It is a life of passion, love, kindness, generosity, happiness and joy"*

Some of us may procrastinate when seeking balance because we believe that balance is based upon someone else or a change in our circumstances.We say, "I'll be able to achieve balance when…I win the lottery, my husband starts helping around the house," or "When I get a new job." etc. Our circumstances shouldn't define who we are.

Balance is truthful, and personal and can be achieved one moment at a time. And it can be found within each of us.We are the only ones who have the power to achieve balance in a way that is meaningful to each of us individually.

CHAPTER 9
BALANCE TAKES PRACTICE

The old English axiom – "practice makes perfect" is true for all of us, from piano students to Olympian athletes.It stands to reason that if high wire acrobats need to practice staying balanced, that same approach makes sense when *we* work to achieve life balance.

Determination and the willingness to continue practicing are also keys to our success.Little children are perfect examples of this idea. Ruth and Brenda remember observing their little ones as they began taking their first steps.

"When our children were learning to walk, we watched them fall, pick themselves back up and try again.They just didn't fear falling.They wanted to walk more than anything.Their little spirits just didn't let them give up.And...they learned how to walk!"

Our lesson here is to regain our determination and commitment to doing something that we believe is so important to us.

There are many ways to accomplish this, but here are a few of our favorites.Add these to your ritual of looking in the mirror and finding things you love about yourself – even if it's your ear lobes!

One practice technique is to make a list of positive attributes using the words, "I am."These two little words are very powerful in that they fuel our beliefs, both positively and negatively.Whenever you use the words, "I am," you are proclaiming who you are to the universe.So, if you say, "I am unsuccessful," or, "I am unlovable," the statements attract these states into your reality.

Use the power of these words to bring what you want in your life into existence."I am happy," and "I am beautiful," are so much more uplifting.Here are a few of ours to get you started.

I am…

- *Kind*
- *A great mom*
- *A devoted friend*
- *Always having fun*
- *A fantastic partner*
- *Healthy and fit*
- *Full of adventure*
- *An engaging speaker*
- *Joyful*
- *Meditating at the beach*
- *Cute as a bug!*

Keep going…

- ______________________________
- ______________________________
- ______________________________
- ______________________________

CHAPTER 10

GOOD NEWS!YOU'RE NOT ALONE!

In 2022, Statista.com published a survey of the number of people in the United States by age and gender.We looked at the number of women from 25 to 60, and there were almost 75 million!While it is impossible to know all of these gals, this statistic proves that we are a mighty group with similar life challenges.

These life challenges differ somewhat, based on the needs of each generation.Millennials (born between 1981 and 1996), Generation X (born between 1965 and 1980) and Baby Boomers (born between 1946 and 1964) have distinct differences, but all women share the common desire to be valued, loved, and happy and share similar concerns of feeling inadequate, overwhelmed, and stuck.

It's so gratifying to know that there are other women "out there" that have the same issues as we do, and the onset of social media has given us opportunities to connect.

Because there is such easy access, women have taken to interacting with others through YouTube videos, Podcasts, Blogs, Instagram, Pinterest, TikTok, and Facebook.

Ruth's daughter Chelsea is a new mom.In preparation for the birth of her daughter, she did research on the Internet and sought out information about pregnancy (she was able to find a lot) and then, once the baby was born, tips and techniques for motherhood.

One of the gals she follows is Jen Hamilton.Jen is married with little ones, and she shares her thoughts and experiences as a wife and mom.One of the reasons that Jen Hamilton is so relatable is that she's honest about her life, both good and bad, and her life experiences show that life is not perfect, but it is so good.

Other great resources for connecting with other women on social media are Facebook, Instagram and Pinterest.It's a great way to connect with people we know and get involved in groups that focus on our interests.

For example, Ruth has recently launched a faith-based book entitled "Giddy Up Estelle!! We've got a lot of living to do!". She has joined several writers' groups that provide a platform for ideas and discussion about writing non-fiction books. While there is great dialogue, it's a bit more difficult to build close relationships. However, in the few short months that she's been involved with her Facebook groups, she has connected with some great gals and become Facebook friends, and they are cheering each other on!

Podcasts have become very popular because women can multi-task, listen to great content and keep on with whatever task they are doing.There are so many and with just a few quick strokes, you can find just about anything you have an interest in. Go for it!

One of the blessings that we have as women, is that we tend to find common ground fairly quickly.Whether you are in your 30's, 40's, 50's or up, it is so important to find your "tribe".

You've probably heard the saying "It takes a village…" The idea of this saying is that we need others in our lives for moral and physical support.We don't want to go through life alone.After all, we've got to share what's happening in our lives with a sister-friend!Who better listens, gives advice, or just hugs you and tells you everything is going to be okay?

Friendships are such a blessing.You never know when you'll meet someone and become fast friends. When Ruth and Brenda first met, they lived in different states.Working for a national company allowed them to connect on a professional level and then later on a personal level.They were both living in Houston at the time their employer sold the company they worked for. They found they had a lot of time on their hands and decided to find a way to continue to live their passion through the writing of the initial version of this book.What a blessing!

The point of this chapter is to encourage you to find opportunities to connect with other women, and share experiences, memories, tips for success, moral support, and laughter.It will do your heart good!

CHAPTER 11
PAY IT FORWARD

Earlier, we mentioned that collectively, we have 3 daughters.Brenda has 1 daughter and Ruth, 2 daughters.We're so proud of the women they have become and asked that they share some of their input on living a life of balance and passion. We asked our daughters questions about balance and passion and what works for them.

Brenda's daughter Kacie is now 32, married with 2 children of her own, and is a partner in a company that provides modern outsourced HR and Recruitment solutions.Here are her thoughts:

1. **What advice would you give to women your age about taking care of yourself?**

To all the women out there, remember that self-care is not a luxury, it is a necessity. Just like the saying goes, "You cannot pour from an empty glass." It is crucial to prioritize your well-being to be the best version of yourself for your loved ones and all aspects of your life.

My non-negotiables are ensuring that I stay hydrated, get 7-8 hours of sleep each night, and have a few meals pre-prepped for the week ahead. These may seem like simple tasks, but they have a profound impact on my overall health and functionality. When I prioritize hydration and adequate rest, I feel more energized, focused, and capable of taking on the many roles I juggle as a mom, boss, wife, and consultant.

2. What are some of your greatest challenges as a working wife and mother?

The greatest challenge is balancing it all without burning yourself (and it all) to the ground. I have come to understand that striving for perfect balance every single day is unrealistic.

Instead, I focus on creating balance over the course of a week. If I find that I am majorly lacking in one area upon reflection of the week, I don't dwell on it or beat myself up, I take proactive steps to address it. I may plan to dedicate more time and attention to that aspect in the following week or day.

3. What is one of your guilty pleasures?

Watching the Taylor Swift Eras Tour over and over!

4. What are you passionate about?

First and foremost, my family is my greatest passion. I am deeply committed to being a nurturing, supportive, and fun mother, creating a safe and loving environment for them to thrive.

Alongside my family, I have a profound passion for supporting small businesses. As an HR consultant specializing in assisting small businesses and busy entrepreneurs, I am dedicated to streamlining their operations, enhancing efficiency, and fostering growth and prosperity. My goal is to make a tangible difference in their lives by providing practical solutions and guidance.

5. What would you love to do if you could?

Dedicate more of my time to volunteering, specifically focusing on assisting mothers who are striving to reenter the workforce. I would love to help them refine their resumes, improve their interview skills, and identify job opportunities that match their aspirations and qualifications.

6. What are some things that you just let go of?

Trying to do it all- I have recently re-read the book, Buying Back Your Time by Dan Martell, and it re-charged my life. Some things are better delegated to someone who can simply get the job done better than you can, even though that can be a tough pill for some of us to swallow.

Ruth's daughter Ashlee is 45, married with two boys and teaches highly gifted elementary age children.She writes reading and writing curriculum for her school district and facilitates a reading program for teachers in the district.Ashlee's story is a bit different in that her two boys are 17 and 3 years old at this writing.She shares her thoughts as a mom to a senior in high school and a toddler.

1. What advice would you give to women your age about taking care of yourself?

Typically, women at my age don't have toddlers.It is an absolute joy in my life to have both my boys, even though their needs are so diverse.I've learned that I have to be purposeful in self-care.For example, I get up before everyone else so that I can have the time to exercise or do whatever else is important to me. I also have joined a group of ladies who work out on Saturday mornings, and I love it!I'm very dedicated to doing this for myself, so I keep the appointment!

2. What are some of your greatest challenges as a working wife and mother?

As a teacher, I pour myself into my students all day, and when I get home, my tank is just about empty.As working moms, we know that the evening will be spent caring for others.Though a joy, it can be exhausting.

3. What is one of your guilty pleasures?

Actually, I have two – getting my nails done or going to the bookstore by myself!

4. What are you passionate about?

I love being an educator.The thrill of helping our young ones excel in their studies and building their character is remarkable.I also cherish my family – my husband, my boys and my very large extended family. Fortunately, we are together often, eating, laughing and enjoying each other's company. I'm so fortunate that we live fairly close to one another and can do this regularly. This helps to fill my cup!

5. What would you love to do if you could?

I would love to travel to a tropical environment and just enjoy the sights and sounds, delicious food and relaxation!

6. What are some things that you just let go of?

I've learned that it's okay to have a messy house every now and then.It's okay to walk away from the dishes and do them later.Teenagers and toddlers can be messy!

Ruth's daughter Chelsea is 36, married, a mother to a little girl with a baby boy on the way.Her husband travels extensively with his work, so she often plays both roles of mom and dad.She is a professional actor and teaches voice and acting lessons to both adults and children.Her career is both fulfilling and challenging as she works sporadic hours.Her career as an actor requires her to audition for every role, which can be daunting.However, she has learned to be happy with "her best" regardless of the outcome of auditions.

1. What advice would you give to women your age about taking care of yourself?

It's so hard to take time for yourself, but you cannot pour from an empty cup. (Sound familiar?) As someone with a non-traditional career, I find that making rest a priority (often a struggle) and a good therapist on speed dial is helpful!Having someone who is impartial, and a willing listener gives you an opportunity to share your struggles and discuss strategies to overcome them.

2. What are some of your greatest challenges as a working wife and mother?

The greatest challenge I face is the balance between work, life, partnership and motherhood.As women who hold these roles, it's fascinating the way we can multitask, but we so often leave little space for the solo human we are.Balancing it all is a real challenge.

3. What is one of your guilty pleasures?

My number one guilty pleasure is reality TV, such as Real Housewives .I love a good escape, especially as an actor who can see twists and turns a mile away.

4. What are you passionate about?

I'm passionate about a lot of things. My family is paramount. But alternatively, I am very passionate about women and their rights and their value and place in society.

5. What would you love to do if you could?

If I could, I would love to have time to go on a trip that is longer than two days. Maybe somewhere with beautiful culture and an even more memorable menu!

6. What are some things that you just let go of?

Something I just let go of was the woman I thought I would be when I crafted my life at 10 years old. Everyone is on their own timeline, has different life experiences and the expectations of others are none of your business.

Thanks, girls!Well said!

You've probably encountered some of the same issues that Kacie, Ashlee and Chelsea have.These struggles are real!The good news, however, is that we can enjoy moments that are fueled by our passions.They don't have to be huge; they just need to be cherished by us.

Take a few minutes to consider your responses to the questions we posed to the girls and consider these suggestions as ideas that you may want to implement.

- Self-care is not a luxury; it is a necessity.
- Daily life balance is very difficult.Strive for weekly balance.
- Avoid beating yourself up when things don't go as planned.
- Let go of trying to do it all.
- Be purposeful in self-care.
- It is okay to have a messy house sometimes.
- Make rest a priority – you can't pour from an empty cup.
- Share your struggles with someone who can be impartial.
- Let go of who you thought you would be and enjoy who you are.

As you read their thoughts, you will notice that though they have similar struggles, they have found ideas that work for them, individually.That is the important distinction here.We have to identify what works for each of us.There may be some trial and error here, but it is so important to find ways to feed your spirit!

Finally, we (Ruth and Brenda) have realized that our children observe us all the time and often develop traits or thoughts that reflect our own as they grow up. Our hope and prayer is that they choose to embody the positive qualities they see in us. This may seem a bit overwhelming, but what a beautiful goal to have as a mom.

Final Thoughts:

- Do not let a situation in one part of your life drain the color, happiness, or passion out of another part of your life.- ***Kacie***

- When you're living a passionate life, you can find joy in the little things when your fire is at the center of it all.- ***Chelsea***

- Always look for the positive in every situation. When you give to others, that kindness brings joy to all those who are involved.- ***Ashlee***

Why don't you take just a moment to jot down your thoughts about how you can treat yourself!You're worth it!

____

____

____

____

CHAPTER 12
LET THE VACUUM KEEP THE CAPE!

Throughout the book, we've talked about the problems that we can wear the cape is satisfying on a metaphoric level, the real issue is not that the suction of the world is pulling at our image, it is the general emptiness we feel when all we are is who we are as Wonder Woman, a character defined by other's expectations.

We know better, down deep inside.The real woman that we are shows up in our higher moments when our true selves emerge without the cape and the bracelets, just holding the lasso of truth.

That gal is not depressed – every choice she makes, a word of encouragement, or support she utters comes from a place of pure authenticity, grounded in her purpose.

The question then becomes, "How do we spend our lives in our 'real woman's' fuzzy slippers, instead of those treacherous, red, high-heeled boots?"You're going to hate the answer – it amounts to letting go.

We all have a true self that emerges in our higher moments, free from the external influences that shape our character. This is the real woman that we are, unencumbered by the cape and the bracelets, and simply holding the lasso of truth. She is not weighed down by depression and lives with authenticity, grounded in her purpose.

The question is, how do we live our lives as our true selves, instead of the persona we have created? The answer is simple but challenging - we must let go. Letting go is not an action, but a state of being. To become who we were meant to be, we must first remove the external expectations that hold us back. We have to welcome the vacuum, and even go as far as to stuff that cape deep inside that hose."

Think of a time when you let go of something and you felt as if a weight had been lifted off your shoulders.Who would ever think that Wonder Woman's cape could be so heavy?

As a woman, you already trust your intuition and intuitively you already know you need to let go - or you wouldn't have bought this book.The title wouldn't have resonated.And you're not alone!So many women have just read the title and said, "Oh my gosh!That's about me!I have to read the book!"

When Marston created Wonder Woman, he recognized the need for vulnerability.And, as we talked about these vulnerabilities in Chapter 8, we realized it is our very vulnerability that makes us human and makes our character important.It is because we cannot do everything that we owe to ourselves and those we love to make purposeful choices.Not out of a hero's need to control the plot of the story, but rather to do the right things even if it costs us the perfect plot, the fairy tale ending.So how do you do that?How do you let go?

The Serenity Prayer - *God grant me the serenity to accept the things I cannot change; courage to change the things I can, and wisdom to know the difference - ends with a request for discernment.*Letting go is not nearly as hard when you know it's the right thing to do.

When we are in our highest self, we can see these truths.At every other instance in our lives, it pays to have people who love us tell us the truth.Not because of their desire to control our plot, but because of their confidence in our character.

It boils down to choice, and that's the hardest part.We often choose to behave in a certain way because of what we believe people need from us.Here's a great exercise that will help you uncover the truth of your beliefs about others' needs.

List important people in your life and then honestly respond to these questions:

1. What do I do based on what I *think* he/she needs?
2. What does he/she need from me?
3. What do I want to be in his/her life?

Chances are, there will be some level of disconnect between what we believe someone needs from us and what he or she really needs.This exercise will involve some good conversations and some of them may be hard.But it will be entirely worth the effort.Remember, focus on the *being* not just the *doing*.Before donning the tiara, the cape, and those treacherous boots, let the vacuum have the cape, not you!

We can't go without sharing some more wonderful insights from women around the world.

Lisa H from Ashville, NC offers a great perspective on the Wonder Woman ideal and what she hopes to share with her daughters.

"I would say though I agree with the fact that the 'Wonder Woman' ideal is damaging - I would also agree that it has brought women to a point in time where they feel more inspired and capable than ever before. Perhaps the pendulum needs to swing in the other direction before it balances out. I do agree that maybe our idea of what "Wonder Woman" really is somewhat backward. She is a woman that is at peace with herself, her path and I would add that she takes care of herself and is confident in who she is. I don't feel that running oneself ragged to the point of ill health is so "Wonder Woman"-ish.

I think that ideal is the remnants of the past of what Women were expected to be. As my daughters grow into the next decade, I hope that they will learn from the past and become a more "whole" woman. To be a true "Wonder Woman" and realize that being confident and loving yourself is what makes you so powerful and beautiful! The perfect image is so much an issue now with how women act and look, and I hope that somehow, I can dilute that image with my own daughters and help them see that perfect is what is inside."

Joanne W. of British Columbia, Canada shared this perspective -

> *"As a personal life coach, who specialized in women in overwhelm, I am always amazed at how women still believe there is no way out, other than to do it all themselves. Historically, they have been taught (or mentored) that women must care for others before them. Recently I attended a celebration event that honored the "superwoman" of the year. What was even more surprising to me was that the event was sponsored by a Canadian organization, headed by women in their 30's. It goes to show that the "belief" of the superwoman still prevails. As a woman in mid-life, I no longer hail the superwoman's icon as something to aspire to. Life's experiences have taught me to take stock of what fulfills my needs and innate values and do more of that. By filling up "my cup" first, I can be of more value and offer more time and energy to those people and things I love and hold dear to me.*
>
> *This has been a great lesson for me personally; as I grew up thinking that the superwomen climbed the "ladder of respect, recognition, love, and career", etc. much faster. However, with too much energy being expended on things that are not a priority in our lives, we can end up burnt out. How valuable are we now?"*

You know, Diana Prince, Wonder Woman's alter ego, dressed more often than not in regular street clothes.She only became Wonder Woman when she needed to be.

Let's take a lesson from her.She found a way to balance her Wonder Woman identity *and* her Wonderous Woman identity.We define a Wonderous Woman as one who knows her truth, takes time to dream, experiences joy, and celebrates her accomplishments, no matter how big or small.

> *"We have overstretched our personal boundaries and forgotten that true happiness comes from living an authentic life fueled with a sense of purpose and balance."*
>
> ***Dr. Kathleen Hall***

Wonderous Woman Characteristics

Throughout the book, we've touched upon five key characteristics of a Wonderous Woman.These characteristics can be summarized by using the acronym DREAM.We developed this acronym because sometimes it is just easier for us to remember things that way!

D - Dream – We live longer, and our spirits are healthier when we dream.It's never too late to begin dreaming!

R - Recognize Your Passions – Passions are clues to your purpose.If time and money weren't in the equation, what would you want to do or have in your life?

E - Experience Joy – The word experience involves sensations that are triggered by things like tasting, feeling, and being. Joy is pure bliss!What brings you joy?Find ways to incorporate more joy in your life.Warning – Experiencing joy may cause a tingling sensation!

A - Affirm Yourself – We were divinely made and there is no one like us in the world. Celebrate who you are and remember to love yourself. Remind yourself about the characteristics that you love about yourself every day.

M - Manifest the Desires of Your Heart – Thoughts become things.Focus on what you want in your life and say yes to opportunities that take you closer to the desires of your heart.

Now What?

It's time for you to write the ending. No, actually the beginning.You cannot move to the next level without letting go of something else.Did you know that New Year's resolutions are the least kept promises?It's because we tend to set huge resolutions, and they become so overwhelming that we just decide to forget about them.

Let's avoid that trap and pick one thing that you can let go of.Think of something each week to let go of and continue until you're empty of the things that are not good for your spirit.

Now get started!

Week one:I'm letting go of ...

____

Week two:I'm letting go of ...

____

Week three: I'm letting go of ...

____

Week four:I'm letting go of ...

____

Keep developing your list as long as it takes to fill the void with the choices made by a uniquely Wonderous Woman.

Before we let you go, we'd like to share the following poem with you.

Not All Heroes Wear Capes

Not all heroes wear capes,
Some wear dresses, jeans and smiles,

Every day they walk among us,
Through life's uncertain miles.

They don't need a badge or uniform,
Or a platform to take a stand,
For their strength is inside their souls, and
In the touch of a loving hand.

They're the wives, mothers, sisters, friends,
Who lift us when we fall,
The ones who stand next to us,
In life's biggest and smallest call.

Life's trials have developed their wisdom,
And their grace softly glows,
They light the darkest pathways,
With the courage that they show.

In every act of kindness,
In every expression of grace,
They can mend hearts that are broken,
Their power lies in love's embrace.

So, to all heroes who don't wear capes,
Who live life with a quiet grace,
They may not be able to move mountains,
But their impact leaves a trace.

It is our heart's desire now that you have finished reading this book, that you will be reacquainted with the girl you are inside, encouraged to nurture your passions and dreams, find balance among the roles you love - and send Wonder Woman back to the comic books!We hope you make a conscious decision every day to make time for the Wonderous Woman you are.

NOTES:

NOTES:

Made in the USA
Middletown, DE
08 February 2025

71015204R00064